THE
CHAD MINDSET
Build the Mind That Can't Be Broken

Logan Creed

Table of Contents

INTRODUCTION

Why You're Failing — And Why It's Not Your Fault (But Still Your Responsibility)

You're not broken. You're just misled. Raised on cheap dopamine, weak leadership, and a system that rewards comfort and punishes discipline. From the moment you were handed a smartphone, you were handed a leash. And since then, everything—from the food you eat to the content you consume—has been engineered to keep you quiet, distracted, and passive. You were never taught to fight. You were taught to comply.

No one told you that manhood isn't something you grow into just by aging. It's forged—through discomfort, through accountability, through mastery. And right now, if you're reading this, it's probably because deep down, you feel like something's off. Like you could be more. Should be more. But you don't know where to start—or you've started but always stall out halfway. That's not laziness. That's a system doing exactly what it was designed to do: keep you average.

Let's get something straight: this book isn't about becoming a Chad in the meme sense. This isn't about becoming an Instagram alpha or throwing out cheesy pickup lines. The Chad Mindset is about reclaiming your agency. It's about the *inner shift*—from reactive to intentional, from weak to disciplined, from confused to clear. It's about rewiring how you think, how you train, how you move through the world. It's a blueprint for becoming the kind of man others respect, but more importantly, the kind of man you respect when you're alone with your thoughts.

You're going to read things in this book that sting. Some chapters will call you out. Others will press on the wounds you've been hiding under distractions, scrolling, porn, cheap food, or short-term wins. You're not here for comfort. You're here because comfort has failed you. You've tried feeling better. Now it's time to *be* better.

And no—your failures aren't entirely your fault. You were handed bad tools. You were told to sit still, behave, wait your turn, trust authority, follow the path. That path led nowhere. But here's the hard truth: now that you know the system is broken, staying broken is on you. You can't keep blaming your past, your parents, your ex, your job, or your mood. You can't control how you got here, but from this point on, everything is your responsibility. Every thought. Every choice. Every outcome.

Responsibility isn't a punishment. It's power. Once you claim it, you start to see results. You stop begging life to treat you better and start becoming someone who demands more—through action, not entitlement. You stop chasing confidence and start building competence. You stop talking about your potential and start earning it. The Chad Mindset begins there—not in hype or hustle porn, but in radical ownership of your time, your habits, your environment, your relationships, your body, and your mind.

This isn't a book you skim. It's one you use. Each chapter will challenge you, then arm you. You'll get clear frameworks for thinking sharper, training harder, living cleaner, leading better. You'll get uncomfortable truths, but also tools to rise above them. You'll stop asking "How do I stay motivated?" and start asking "What needs to be done?"

By the end of this book, if you show up and do the work, you'll have a new operating system. One that's built not on hype, but on hardened self-respect. You'll stop living like a passenger and start acting like the driver. You'll stop living day-to-day and start living with a mission. You were made for more. And the world won't hand it to you. You'll have to take it. One rep, one decision, one day at a time.

Welcome to *The Chad Mindset*. Let's get to work.

PART I: RECLAIM YOUR MIND

The War Starts in Your Head

Every day you wake up, you enter a battle—not against the world, not against other men, but against yourself. That voice that tells you to hit snooze, to skip the workout, to "do it tomorrow"—that's your enemy. It wears your face. It sounds like you. And if you don't learn how to recognize it, fight it, and silence it, it will own your life. Most men never get that far. They blame the external—money, time, women, society—when the real enemy has been living in their skull from the beginning.

You've got two voices. One wants your comfort. The other wants your growth. The comfort voice is seductive. It speaks softly, offers justifications, gives you permission to quit. "You've worked hard already," it says. "Just one more hour of sleep. One more scroll. You'll start tomorrow." But that voice lies. Every time you listen to it, you lose ground. You reinforce the habit of giving in. It gets stronger. Quieter, but stronger. Until one day you don't even hear it— you just act on it, automatically, like a puppet.

The other voice—the one calling you to move, to train, to do the hard thing even when you don't feel like it—that one's weaker at first. It doesn't scream. It whispers. And you'll only hear it if you learn to shut the other one up. That's the start of the war: identifying which voice is which. You don't have to be perfect. You don't have to win every time. But the more reps you put in—catching yourself before the excuse wins, overriding it with action—the easier it becomes to choose the stronger path.

This war happens in moments. It's not some dramatic movie montage. It's subtle. You're on the couch. The gym bag is five feet away. You know you need to go. But there's friction. A pause. A negotiation. That's the battleground. That pause is your chance. If you act in that space, you win. If you delay, you lose. The more you act without negotiation, the more you train your brain to obey your highest intention—not your lowest impulse.

Self-talk matters. It's not just what you say when you're motivated. It's what you say when you're tired, alone, frustrated. Do you say, "I've failed again," or do you say, "Not today. We're still in the fight"? Do you say, "I always mess up," or "I slipped, but I don't stop"? You're not just speaking, you're programming. Every sentence you let loop in your mind is code. The question is whether you're coding a coward or a killer.

And yes, it's going to hurt. Growth always does. Your brain doesn't want you to change. It wants efficiency. Routine. Safety. That's why breaking bad habits feels like withdrawal. It's psychological friction. But if you reframe that pain—as progress, as proof that you're changing the wiring—you stop running from it. You lean into it. And you start building momentum.

The Chad Mindset isn't about being fearless. It's about doing what needs to be done even when the fear is loud. It's about showing up to the fight inside your head and throwing punches when you'd rather hide. The more often you do that, the more you train yourself to be the kind of man who acts despite emotion, who moves despite doubt, who chooses growth even when it sucks. This is how you win the war—not in a single battle, but in thousands of tiny, private victories that no one sees. Waking up early when no one's watching. Saying no to that distraction. Finishing the set. Making the call. Writing the plan. Sitting in discomfort instead of escaping. These aren't just habits. They're weapons. Use them.

You want to become stronger? Start here. In your mind. In your decisions. In your ability to separate the weak voice from the true one. Your mind is the battlefield. You either own it, or it owns you. Decide.

Building Grit, Focus & Stoic Strength

"You have power over your mind —
not outside events. Realize this, and you
will find strength."
— Marcus Aurelius

Mental toughness isn't something you're born with. It's not a genetic gift or a personality type. It's trained — through tension, repetition, and discomfort. Just like building muscle, you have to break the old fibers to grow new ones. That process isn't clean or pleasant. It's gritty. It hurts. But that's the price of becoming solid — not just on the outside, but deep in your mind where it actually matters.

Most men are fragile, not because they're weak by nature, but because they've never had to face real resistance. Everything around them is designed to soften them — comfort food, instant rewards, curated dopamine on demand. The modern world teaches you to avoid discomfort at all costs. But here's the truth: **comfort is killing your edge**. The only way to get it back is to lean into the hard stuff — deliberately, repeatedly, and without apology.

Hard by Choice

Start with the simple things. Cold exposure is a perfect example. Cold showers, ice baths, standing outside shirtless in winter air. Not because it's trendy. Because it's *training*. When you step into freezing water, your body panics. Your brain screams to get out. But you don't. You breathe through it. You stay calm in chaos. And that's not just physical — it's mental dominance. You're teaching yourself that fear doesn't get to decide anymore.

"If you can endure discomfort voluntarily, you can endure anything involuntarily."

The more you voluntarily do hard things, the more you teach your nervous system: we're in control. That's where grit is born — not in the absence of fear or pain, but in your ability to meet it and say, "Not today."

Repetition matters. One cold shower won't change your life. But a hundred will. Not because of the cold, but because of what you become through the act of choosing it over and over. You become the kind of man who doesn't need to feel ready to take action. That's the foundation of discipline.

Write Like a Warrior

Journaling isn't just a mental health tool — it's tactical. It sharpens self-awareness like a blade. Most men drift through life with no real grasp of what's driving them, what's holding them back, or what patterns they're stuck in. Writing cuts through the noise. It gives form to thoughts, exposes excuses, and gives you a real-time audit of your inner battlefield.

Don't write like a victim. Write like a warrior planning a campaign. What worked today? What broke down? Where did you slip? Where did you win? How will you adjust? It's not about venting — it's about gaining clarity. The better you understand yourself, the more precisely you can act. That's real focus — not just staring at a screen for hours, but aligning action with direction.

Emotions Under Pressure

Emotional control isn't about suppression — it's about mastery. It's being able to sit in the heat of anger, fear, rejection, or stress and not let it own you. Too many men live like waves in a storm — up and down, tossed around by whatever hits them that day. But the men who lead, the men who others trust, the men who get things done — they stay anchored.

That doesn't mean they feel nothing. It means they feel it, then choose what to do with it. That's the difference between reaction and response. One is emotional reflex. The other is power. Every time you choose to pause, breathe, and act with clarity instead of rage or panic, you're reinforcing strength.

So let that be your measure. What throws you off? What pulls you down? What do you give your energy to without realizing it? If everything riles you, you're not strong — you're reactive. Your enemy will always use your emotions against you if you don't own them first.

The Stoic Triad

The Stoics knew this war long before you did. They lived in times of war, exile, betrayal, and death — and they developed a mindset forged in those flames. The Stoic triad is brutally simple: **Control what you can. Endure what you must. Ignore the rest.**

Most men waste 80% of their energy on things they can't control — what others think, what might happen, what went wrong in the past. That's weakness disguised as concern. Strength is choosing to focus only on what's in your hands. Your training. Your words. Your responses. Your habits. Your daily wins. That's your kingdom. Rule it, or be ruled by everything else.

"He who angers you controls you. He who distracts you defeats you."

When you live by that code, your energy sharpens. You stop leaking it through gossip, overthinking, and victim talk. You become precise. Tactical. Calm under fire. That's the kind of man others follow — not the loudest, but the clearest.

Repetition Builds the Real You

None of this works once. It works when it becomes who you are. That's the whole point of mental reps. Every time you do something hard on purpose, every time you override emotion with discipline, every time you sit down to journal, every time you hold the line when chaos hits — you're reinforcing the man you're becoming.

That man isn't motivated. He's trained. That man doesn't need hype. He's wired. That man doesn't need the world to go his way. He adapts, endures, and moves forward no matter what.

And that's where you're heading — not toward perfection, but toward power. Quiet, durable, unshakable power. Not the kind that flexes online, but the kind that carries weight when it's time to show up in real life.

So do your reps. Build your mind like you build your body. Show up daily. Embrace friction. Think clearly. Respond with purpose. Ignore the noise. Because the world doesn't need more noise. It needs men who can keep their head while everyone else is losing theirs.

"Suffer the pain of discipline, or suffer the pain of regret."

You decide.

Dopamine Detox and Digital Discipline

You don't need more willpower. You need less noise.

Your brain was never built for this level of stimulation. It evolved for survival, problem-solving, movement, tension, and human connection. But now it's drowning in artificial signals, engineered distractions, and hyper-fast rewards. You wake up and reach for your phone before your feet hit the ground. You're getting hit with likes, messages, updates, images, headlines — all before you've even taken your first breath of real air. This has become normal, and that's the problem.

It's not your fault. You were born into this system. But it *is* your responsibility to wake up from it. Right now, your attention span is fractured. You can't sit still for more than five minutes without checking something. You get frustrated easily. You avoid hard things even when you know they matter. And it's not because you're lazy — it's because your brain is overstimulated and under-trained. The enemy isn't just procrastination. It's the environment you've unconsciously allowed to hijack your mind.

The worst part? You barely notice it happening.

You feel tired even when you haven't done anything. You feel restless but can't explain why. You want to change but can't stay consistent. You keep chasing motivation, but nothing sticks. That's not a discipline problem. That's a *dopamine problem*. The wiring is off.

Your brain runs on reward. And right now, it's getting flooded with rewards you didn't earn. Easy ones. Scrolls, swipes, porn, sugar, clickbait, fake progress. Your body sits still, your mind goes nowhere, but your brain thinks you've accomplished something because it got the hit. Over time, this breaks the drive to pursue real goals. They feel slow. Boring. Too difficult. That's what dopamine saturation does — it rewrites your perception of effort and reward.

This is the war. Not just against screens or porn or YouTube rabbit holes. It's a war for your attention, your motivation, your fire. You can't win it with hacks. You win it by cutting the leash and building your own system. A system that restores your baseline, rebuilds your focus, and reintroduces the power of *earned* dopamine.

Cut the Leash, Face the Void

Start with your phone. Track your screen time without flinching. Look at where your hours go. Not what you *think* you do, but what you *actually* do. Social media. Short videos. Meaningless tabs open all day. Constant checking. Most of it isn't serving you. It's sedating you. And it's keeping you from the things you claim you care about.

The idea isn't to go full monk and disappear. The idea is to use tools without being used by them. That means turning your phone into a weapon, not a pacifier. It means creating rules — non-negotiable ones. No phone in bed. No notifications except for actual emergencies. No back-to-back dopamine loops. No content while eating. These small changes add up fast. Each one creates friction against the impulse. Each one makes you slightly more *aware*. And awareness is the beginning of freedom.

Now we have to talk about porn — and you already know why.

It's the most common, most normalized, most destructive habit in modern male life. And it's not just about sex. It's about the wiring. Every time you open a tab, scroll through thumbnails, chase novelty, and finish with a dopamine spike, your brain logs it as an achievement. Your biology rewards you for nothing. No effort, no connection, no risk, no intimacy. Just dopamine. Over and over. The cost? You start to feel less. Care less. Desire less. You lose tension. You lose drive. You lose your edge. It happens slowly — until the moment you need to act like a man, and you feel like a ghost instead.

Porn isn't harmless. It weakens you. And quitting it is hard because your system has been trained to rely on it for emotional release, boredom relief, and temporary escape. But withdrawal is part of the cure. And the discomfort you feel when you quit? That's the friction that resets your baseline. That's the mind rebalancing. It sucks — but so does being a slave to your own cravings.

Delete it. Block it. Cut the access points. Break the routine. And then sit in the tension. Don't numb it — use it. Channel it. Let it become fuel for action. That energy doesn't go away — it just needs a place to go. If you don't give it one, it will go back to what's familiar. Once you begin removing the junk, something strange happens. You start to feel bored.

That's good. That's the space you've been avoiding. That's the silence where your mind can finally breathe. Let it happen. Stop trying to fill every quiet moment. That boredom is training. It's teaching your nervous system how to stay grounded without stimulation. And in that boredom, you'll find focus. You'll feel the pull to work on something real. To train. To create. To be useful.

You don't need more apps. You need more stillness. Not because stillness is peaceful — but because stillness is *unfiltered*. It brings everything to the surface. The distractions, the emotions, the truths you've buried. That's the beginning of mental clarity. You can't fix what you're not willing to feel.

Reset, Rebuild, Reclaim

Once you've cleaned the input, start rebuilding the output.

Get addicted to effort. To training. To delayed gratification. Make your rewards mean something again. Don't scroll to relax — go walk. Don't binge to escape — go write. Don't swipe for validation — go lift. Use your body. Use your mind. Earn your pleasure. Make the reward follow the effort, not the other way around.

And be relentless about your environment. Remove temptation where it lives. Rearrange your apps. Block sites that waste your time. Turn your home into a training ground, not a digital trap. Put books on your desk instead of devices. Set your schedule with intention — and actually follow it. Time is not something you find. It's something you *defend*.

This isn't about becoming a productivity robot. It's about becoming *free*. Free to choose. Free to focus. Free to follow through on what matters without constantly dragging yourself out of distraction hell. You'll never be perfect. That's not the goal. But you can build a system where your defaults support your mission — not sabotage it.

Dopamine isn't the enemy. It's part of your drive. You just need to reset the balance. Earn the spikes. And stop feeding the parts of you that want the shortcut. Every time you delay gratification, you signal strength. Every time you choose friction, you build resilience. Every time you do something difficult instead of something easy, you teach your brain who's really in charge.

This process isn't glamorous. No one claps for you when you shut down YouTube and go for a walk. No one notices when you say no to porn for the fifth time this week. But you notice. You feel it. You grow from it. And slowly, you become the kind of man who doesn't need to be entertained to feel alive.

You'll begin to notice how others are still caught in the loop — always scrolling, always chasing, always tired, always saying they'll start next week. You'll see it clearly because you're no longer inside of it. And that clarity will give you power — the power to lead yourself while the rest of the world gets led by screens.

None of this happens overnight. You'll relapse. You'll slip. You'll have days where the noise wins. That's fine. Just don't let it become your identity again. Every time you get back on track, you win. Every time you sharpen your awareness and act in spite of craving, you reinforce the path forward. And over time, that becomes your baseline — not distraction, not impulse, but direction.

Discipline is not about saying no forever. It's about saying no *until you're ready to say yes to something better*. And the longer you hold the line, the more powerful your yes becomes. The more clear your thoughts become. The more intense your drive becomes. You stop faking motivation and start operating from purpose.

Kill the noise. Cut the leash. Get your fire back.
This is your mind. Own it.

PART II: BUILD YOUR BODY

Earn Respect in the Mirror

You know what it feels like to avoid the mirror.

That glance you catch when you're brushing your teeth, passing a window, changing your shirt — and something in you looks away just a little too quickly. You don't want to look, because looking means facing it. The softness. The slouch. The version of you that isn't showing up fully. It's not about how you look to others. It's about how you look to *yourself*.

And deep down, you know exactly why the reflection doesn't feel right. You know you've been neglecting the body you were given. You've been putting it last. You've let it lose tension, lose fire, lose the sharpness that makes a man walk into a room with weight behind him. And even if no one else can see it, *you* can. Every morning. Every night. The mirror doesn't care about your excuses. It just shows you the truth.

This isn't about vanity. This isn't about likes or compliments. This is about respect — and not the kind you get from others. The kind that only exists when you've earned it from *yourself*.

When you look in the mirror and know you've been showing up, pushing yourself, doing hard things when it was easier to make excuses — there's a quiet power in that. You don't need to talk about it. You don't need to prove anything. You just *know*. And that knowing bleeds into everything: how you speak, how you stand, how you move, how you carry yourself around other people. They feel it. But more importantly, *you* feel it.

There's a spiritual weight to physical training. Because every time you make the decision to train — especially when you don't feel like it — you're reinforcing the idea that you're a man who does what must be done. Not for a reward. Not for praise. But because it's your standard.

That's where real confidence is born — not in achieving some perfect body, but in the process of repeatedly doing something hard, uncomfortable, and painful... without needing a reason beyond *this is what I do.* You don't need to be shredded to earn your own respect. But you do need to stop running from discomfort. You do need to start moving like a man who values himself. You do need to build a body that's ready to carry the weight of your goals, your responsibilities, your mission. Because if your body is falling apart, don't lie to yourself — *so is your discipline.*

Strength Is a Language

Your body speaks before you do.

You might not realize it, but people form their opinion of you in the first few seconds based entirely on how you carry yourself. And if you carry yourself like a man who doesn't take care of his body, you're sending a loud message — even if you're silent.

Your posture, your presence, your energy — they all come from the way you've trained (or haven't). A man who's built his body through years of consistent training moves differently. He doesn't need to puff his chest or raise his voice. He doesn't need to dominate the room. He's already felt pain and chosen to keep going. That confidence settles in the way he walks, the way he listens, the way he stands still.

Strength is a language. And everyone around you speaks it, whether they realize it or not. When you train regularly, when you push your limits physically, when you sweat and suffer and stay with it — something hardens inside you. You stop flinching at discomfort. You stop backing down from hard conversations. You stop doubting yourself every time things don't go your way. Because deep down, you know what you're capable of. You've seen it in the mirror. You've felt it under a heavy bar. You've watched it grow over time.

And when you *know* you're capable, you move through life with a different tempo. Not rushed. Not reactive. Not needing to prove anything. Just steady, grounded, present. That presence changes how others treat you. But more importantly, it changes how *you* treat yourself.

Here's the truth: people don't treat you based on your potential. They treat you based on your presentation. You could have the biggest heart in the world, but if you look like you've given up on yourself, don't expect people to hand you respect. You have to show — through your discipline, your energy, your body — that you value yourself enough to put in the work.

The men who train with purpose aren't just building muscle. They're building *proof.*

Proof that they can commit. Proof that they can endure. Proof that they can finish what they start. When you've trained through the pain, through boredom, through plateaus, through bad weeks and good times, that proof becomes your armor. Not arrogance — just conviction. Quiet conviction. And that's what makes the mirror change. Not the muscle. Not the aesthetics. The *meaning* behind the change. When you know what it took to earn the body you see, every glance at your reflection becomes a reminder: I didn't quit. I'm not soft. I'm still building. I'm still in the fight. That's a man worth respecting.

Train For Character, Not Just Physique

Forget the perfect program. Forget the supplements. Forget the TikTok fitness hacks. What you need more than anything is consistency and discomfort — nothing fancy, just brutally simple effort over time. You train to become *useful*, not impressive. You train to become the kind of man who can lead under pressure, protect others, stay grounded in chaos, and follow through when it's hard.

That kind of man is rare. Not because the workouts are complicated, but because the mindset behind them is misunderstood. Too many men train for looks, for validation, for attention — and when that fades, they quit. But when you train for character, for grit, for presence, you never run out of reasons to keep going. It becomes your code.

If you can move your body every single day — not just when it's easy, not just when you're motivated — you're reinforcing something far more important than muscle. You're reinforcing the idea that you can trust yourself.

And that trust will bleed into your work, your relationships, your decisions. You won't have to hype yourself up to do what's necessary. You'll already be trained for it. You'll be sharp, ready, focused. You'll feel it in the way you wake up, the way you walk, the way you say no to things that used to own you. The discipline you build in the gym — or the street, or your room, or the park — is the same discipline you'll use when everything else in life starts falling apart. It's your foundation. And you'll need it more than you think.

Start where you are. Bodyweight training. Long walks. Cold showers. Sprints. Push-ups. Pull-ups. Heavy carries. You don't need a gym, just the will to begin. If you train like your life depends on it, you'll start living like a man who deserves the life he's chasing. And after six months of that — not perfect, not always motivated, but *relentless* — you'll look in the mirror and feel something shift. It won't be pride. It'll be peace. Because you'll know you're no longer lying to yourself.

You'll see a man who's not just building a body — he's building a *code*. And once you earn respect in the mirror, no one can take that from you.

Tactical Training: The Chad Body Blueprint

You don't need a gym membership. You don't need fancy supplements or influencers shouting rep ranges at you. What you need is a system — a clear, simple, unbreakable system that makes training part of who you are, not something you try to squeeze in when you "have time." Because time isn't found. It's made. And if your body isn't a priority now, it never will be.

The truth is, most men don't fail because they don't know *how* to train. They fail because they train without purpose. They move without direction. They chase random workouts, follow trends, and lose focus as soon as life gets busy. What you need is not another "plan." You need a *framework* that trains your body and mind as one — built to make you harder, faster, more focused, more capable. Not for summer. For life.

The Chad Body Blueprint isn't about bodybuilding or aesthetics. It's about function, consistency, and discipline. It's about owning a body that works under pressure, moves with power, and doesn't quit when everything hurts. You don't have to become a fitness junkie. You just have to stop being fragile.

Your body is your first weapon. Your vehicle. Your armor. If it's weak, everything you build on top of it is unstable. But when it's strong — truly strong — everything else follows. The goal here is simple: build a body that can handle anything, anywhere, with minimal excuses.

This program is designed for men who want results without the fluff — no gyms, no machines, no excuses. Just your body, gravity, and grit. Because when you strip training down to its essentials, that's all you really need.

The Training

The system works on three principles: **consistency, intensity, and adaptability.**

Consistency means showing up no matter what. Even if it's ten minutes. Even if you're tired. Especially when you don't feel like it. The habit matters more than the duration. A short, consistent session done daily will outwork a perfect plan that you quit after two weeks. This system builds momentum by removing decision fatigue. You don't think. You just do.

Intensity means effort, not ego. Every rep should feel like it costs something. You don't have to destroy yourself every session — but you can't coast, either. Training is the time to test your willpower against your comfort zone. If you're not breathing heavy, sweating, and fighting the urge to stop, you're not doing it right. The more you flirt with that line, the stronger your mind becomes.

Adaptability means no excuses. No gym? Fine. No equipment? Fine. Too busy? Split your workout. Too tired? Move anyway. This system scales with your reality. Because the mission isn't to be perfect — it's to be unstoppable. Every obstacle becomes part of the training.

When you live by those three principles, the plan below becomes almost impossible to fail.

The 30-Day Chad Training Blueprint

This 30-day system is built around what I call *The Four Foundations*: Push, Pull, Legs, and Core. Everything you do falls into one of these categories. Together, they build a complete, capable body. You'll train six days a week, rotating through these foundations, with one rest or light movement day per week. Each session should take about 30–45 minutes. Remember always to rest, it's really important for your health and for your training too.

But before you jump in, understand this: **form and effort are your two currencies.** You make progress by mastering both. Every rep counts only if it's done with control. Every session counts only if you give it attention.

Week 1–2: Build the Base

Your mission here is to establish consistency and rhythm. Don't chase numbers yet. Chase habit.

Day 1 – Push (Chest, Shoulders, Triceps) Push-ups (4 sets to failure) Pike Push-ups (3 sets of 10–12) Tricep Dips (on chair or bench, 3 sets of 10–15)
Day 2 – Pull (Back, Biceps) Inverted Rows (under table or bar, 4 sets of 8–12) Chin-ups (assisted if needed, 3 sets of 6–10) Towel Curls (3 sets of 12–15)
Day 3 – Legs (Quads, Glutes, Hamstrings) Squats (4 sets of 20)

Lunges (3 sets of 10 per leg)
Wall Sit (3 rounds of 45 seconds)
Day 4 – Core + Conditioning
Plank (3 sets of 1 minute)
Leg Raises (3 sets of 12–15)
Mountain Climbers (3 rounds, 30 seconds each)
Day 5 – Push
Repeat Day 1, aim for cleaner form or more reps.
Day 6 – Legs + Core
Mix both: Squats, Lunges, Plank, Leg Raises. Push intensity.
Day 7 – Rest or Active Recovery
Walk. Stretch. Move lightly. Reflect on the week.

Week 3–4: Increase the Demand

You've built the rhythm. Now it's time to push the limits. The rules stay the same, but you'll add volume, tension, and intensity.

Add one extra set to each movement.
Shorten rest times to 30–45 seconds.
Add resistance (a backpack with weight, slow tempos, or isometric holds).
Add daily movement: 10,000 steps minimum.

In these final two weeks, your mission is simple — *earn fatigue.* Finish each session knowing you couldn't have done more. This is where you build confidence that translates into everything else.

The Mind Behind the Muscle

This system is about more than building strength — it's about building reliability. Every rep is a small act of proof. Every workout is a promise kept. Every drop of sweat is a reminder that you're in control of your time, your choices, your life.

Training daily will start to bleed into everything you do. You'll eat better because your body craves performance. You'll sleep better because you've earned rest. You'll think more clearly because movement clears the noise. You'll stop second-guessing because you've got evidence: evidence that you're capable of doing hard things and not quitting. That's why you train like your life depends on it. Because in a way, it does. Your future depends on the man you're becoming now — the man who doesn't skip, doesn't hide, doesn't wait. The man who moves, even when no one's watching.

You don't need perfection. You need proof. And every session, every rep, every drop of sweat adds to it. You don't train for looks. You train for life. And when you do, the mirror takes care of itself.

Fuel Like a Warrior, not a Wimp

Real men don't diet. They fuel. They don't count rice grains or track every calorie like they're prepping for a physique competition. They eat like warriors — to build, to recover, to focus, to fight. Food isn't entertainment. It's strategy. It's fuel for the battles you face daily, whether in the gym, in the office, or in your own head. And if you keep eating like a bored teenager on a dopamine bender, you'll keep living like one — soft, tired, foggy, reactive.

This isn't about biohacking. It's not about keto, paleo, or whatever trend is being sold on your feed. This is about timeless, high-performance eating for men who need their bodies and minds to work — hard, often, and without breakdown. You can lift all you want, meditate all you want, read all the self-help books on Earth... but if you're eating like trash, you're building your life on a broken engine.

Food controls your energy. Your energy controls your decisions. Your decisions shape your entire trajectory.

So no, this isn't optional. You don't need a master's in nutrition to get this right. You need common sense and consistency. Your body doesn't need perfection. It needs rhythm. It needs real food at regular times. It needs water, protein, fat, minerals, and movement. That's it. But modern eating has drifted so far from that simplicity that most men think they need apps and tracking spreadsheets just to not feel like crap.

You don't need a spreadsheet. You need *standards,* and to listen to your body. If you keep treating food like a mood fix or a boredom filler, you'll keep digging the same hole. But when you start seeing every meal as a way to sharpen the blade — that's when things change. You stop mindlessly consuming and start *fueling* your next move. You stop chasing cravings and start chasing clarity. You stop relying on stimulants and start eating like a man who actually wants to win the day. Because that's the real point: food isn't the reward. It's the *weapon*.

Eating For Power, Not Perfection

Let's simplify it all. You need protein to build. You need fats to fuel your hormones. You need carbs for performance. You need water like your life depends on it — because it does. And you need to cut the garbage that's been slowly stealing your focus, your drive, and your testosterone.

We're not counting macros. We're not labeling foods good or bad. We're cutting the mental noise. Your meals should be simple, clean, and repeatable. The more friction you remove from the process, the more likely you are to stick with it. You want to build a rhythm so solid you barely have to think. Just like training, the power is in the repetition.

Here's the mission:
— Prioritize whole, single-ingredient foods
— Build meals around protein
— Eat at regular times
— Minimize ultra-processed trash
— Hydrate early, hydrate often
— Don't snack like a boy, eat like a man

This isn't a diet. This is fueling discipline. You're building the kind of body and brain that can stay sharp, move heavy things, and focus for hours without crashing. That doesn't happen on fast food, soda, and sugar. You already know that. You've *felt* that crash. You've felt the fog. You've felt what it's like to be overfed but undernourished. That's what happens when you chase comfort on a plate instead of clarity.

And testosterone? It doesn't survive in a body built on low-fat snacks, high-stress blood sugar spikes, and energy drinks at midnight. If you want to build strength, confidence, presence, and sex drive — start with the food on your plate. Fat, cholesterol, red meat, eggs, salt, water — these aren't enemies. They're fuel. They've kept strong men alive and lethal for centuries. Trust them more than the new "zero-calorie" drink your algorithm's pushing today.

Day Of Fuel + Warrior Hacks

If you're broke or busy, you don't need a custom meal plan. You need a *go-to routine*. Something repeatable, affordable, and hard to mess up.

Here's what a day of high-performance eating could look like. Not perfect. Just powerful.

Wake up: Water — lots of it. Your brain is dehydrated. Before the coffee, chug a tall glass. Add a pinch of salt if you're training hard. Your first win of the day is hydration. Don't skip it.

Breakfast (optional): If you're training early or feeling depleted — eggs, oats, banana, or protein shake with peanut butter.

If you're focused and sharp without eating, skip the meal. Use the fasted clarity and eat later. Know your body.

Lunch: Ground beef, rice, olive oil, vegetables. Simple. Satisfying. Fuel that doesn't slow you down. Add fermented foods like sauerkraut or pickles for gut health. Don't overthink it — you're not trying to impress anyone. You're feeding your mission.

Afternoon: Water again. Salt again. Optional black coffee or green tea if focus dips — not as a crutch, but as a tool. Hard-boiled eggs, greek yogurt, or a protein bar if needed.

Dinner: Steak or chicken thighs, potatoes, greens. Eat to recover. Eat to rebuild. Add avocado or olive oil if you've trained hard. Then stop eating. Give your body time to rest before bed.

Before sleep: Herbal tea. No sugar, no screens, no snacks. Let your brain come down. Respect the recovery process.

Maybe this doesn't look that exciting.... But it *works*. And that's all that matters. You don't have to meal prep for Instagram. You just have to stop winging it. Batch cook rice, meat, and vegetables once or twice a week. Keep eggs, yogurt, and frozen berries stocked. Use a blender when time's tight. Keep salt, olive oil, and seasonings on hand to avoid bland meals. Simplicity is the key to sustainability.

If you're hungry all the time, you're probably sleep-deprived, dehydrated, or eating low-quality carbs. Fix that first. If you're always bloated or foggy, your gut is inflamed. Clean it up. Stop hammering down garbage and expecting high performance.When you fuel right, you recover faster. You think sharper. You stop reaching for sugar because your body is already satisfied. Your cravings fade because you're not chasing dopamine — you're chasing dominance. And that's how you eat like a warrior. Not perfectly. Not obsessively. But *intentionally*. Fuel is focus. Fuel is clarity. Fuel is power.

So from now on, every time you eat, ask yourself one question:

Is this making me stronger or softer? Then choose accordingly.

PART III: SYSTEMS OVER MOTIVATION

Discipline > Motivation: The Non-Negotiables Method

Motivation is that voice in your head that says, "Let's go!" when you're already in a good mood. It shows up when you've slept well, eaten clean, had an easy morning, and maybe watched a hype video or two. But motivation is unreliable. It fades as the second life pushes back — the moment your alarm goes off early, your day gets hard, your energy dips, or your mood shifts.

You've probably had days where you *felt* on fire and promised yourself, you'd change everything. New routines, new habits, clean eating, all of it. You were dead serious... for a few hours. Then you got tired. Distracted. Busy. And by the next morning, the fire was gone. This is why men who rely on motivation always fail — not because they're weak, but because they're building on emotion instead of identity. Discipline is different. Discipline doesn't matter how you feel. Discipline is doing what must be done *especially* when you're not in the mood. Discipline is following through without negotiating with your comfort. It's not sexy. It's not loud. But it wins. Every time.

And here's the best part: discipline isn't some innate personality trait. It's not just "for certain people." It's *built* — through repetition, structure, environment, and friction. You don't wake up one day with a disciplined mind. You construct it — piece by piece — through daily actions that hardwire strength into your routine. The goal isn't to become a robot. The goal is to make your standards *immune* to your feelings.

And that's what non-negotiables do. They turn daily actions into identity. When done consistently, they make quitting feel unnatural — like leaving the house without clothes. Something just feels off when you skip them. That's when you know you're winning.

You're not building discipline for motivation's sake. You're building it so you stop needing motivation altogether.

Lock in Identity

Every man has a self-image — a quiet set of beliefs about who he is and what he does. Most people try to change their behavior without changing that image. That never works. If deep down, you believe you're inconsistent, lazy, or weak, no routine will stick. You'll self-sabotage the second things get hard. The way out? Stack small wins until the image changes.

That starts with action. You don't wait until you *feel* disciplined. You act as if you already are. You don't wait to feel confident before you lead. You lead while scared. You take small, daily actions that align with the man you want to become — and eventually, the mirror starts to reflect that.

Every non-negotiable is a brick in the wall of your future identity. One workout. One cold shower. One clean meal. One day without a dopamine spiral. Each one says: *this is who I am now.* And the longer you hold the line, the more powerful that statement becomes. Discipline isn't just about what you do. It's about what you believe about yourself. When you act with integrity, repeatedly, the belief shifts. You stop needing to hype yourself up. You just know: *I show up. That's what I do.*

Build the Chain

Imagine your daily standards as links in a chain. Every time you hit your non-negotiables, the chain gets longer. You're building momentum, pattern, proof. That streak gives you power. But more importantly, it gives you pressure not to break it. You don't want to "start over." You want to protect what you've already earned.

The idea isn't perfection. You'll miss sometimes. You'll have off days. But the key is *consistency with recovery.* One miss doesn't break you. Letting it spiral does. You miss a day? Fine. Bounce back. Show yourself that the habit lives even after failure. That's real strength.

But when you're on a streak, guard it with everything you have. Because the longer that chain gets, the stronger your identity becomes. And eventually, showing up becomes automatic. You'll hit your habits without thinking. You won't need reminders. You won't need hype. You'll just do the work — because that's what the chain does.

Like This

You don't need a thousand habits. You need a few *non-negotiables* — high-impact actions that align your daily behavior with your long-term mission. These are the habits that move the needle. They're small enough to do even on bad days, but powerful enough to keep you on the path.

A few examples:

- Wake up at a consistent time.
- Move your body every day.
- Drink a full glass of water upon waking.
- Journal for five minutes before bed.
- Stay off social media before noon.
- Make your bed with intention.
- Stretch or cold shower after training.
- Plan your next day before you sleep.

These aren't just rituals. They're proof. Every time you do them, you're telling yourself: *I lead myself. I don't need emotion to act.* That's the seed of unbreakable discipline. The best non-negotiables are simple. You don't have to force them. They fit your life. They don't drain your willpower — they reinforce it. And over time, they shape your day so tightly that there's no space left for weakness to take hold. You don't need to be perfect. But you need to be relentless. Hit your non-negotiables like your life depends on it — because your future does.

Hard Days Matter More

Anyone can show up when it's easy. The difference is made on the hard days — when you're tired, uninspired, overwhelmed, or pissed off. Those are the days that define your trajectory. That's where the gap between amateurs and killers widens.

The men who show up on hard days build something unshakable. The workout doesn't have to be great. The journaling doesn't have to be profound. The meal doesn't have to be clean and perfect. What matters is that you *don't fold*. You protect the baseline. You do *something* — even if it's just a rep. And that act — choosing to move through resistance instead of waiting for it to pass — is where real identity gets built. When you look back at those days and realize you didn't quit, you gain a different kind of confidence. Not the loud, performative kind. The quiet, durable kind.

You want to trust yourself? Then earn that trust when it's hardest to give.

Like This

Structure gives you freedom.

People think freedom means waking up whenever you want, doing whatever feels good, living without rules. But that's not freedom — that's slavery to impulse. Real freedom is knowing your day before it begins. It's building such a tight system that you don't waste time deciding what to do. You just *do*. You can still be flexible. You can adjust. But you have a spine now — a frame that holds your life together no matter what chaos is around you. That's what structure does. It becomes your armor. You don't need to "try" to stay focused. Your environment and your habits carry you. The goal isn't rigidity. The goal is stability. If your schedule collapses every time life throws something new at you, you don't have a life — you have a reaction. The disciplined man is adaptable. But his core doesn't move.

Discipline is the Death of Doubt

When you've kept your promises long enough, something dies inside you — the part of you that doubts. The part that says "maybe," the part that waits for permission, the part that fears failure.

Discipline kills that voice.

Because once you've proven to yourself that you can show up every day, even when it sucks, you stop questioning whether you're capable. You stop negotiating. You start *moving.* And with every rep, every journal page, every clean meal, every cold shower, you chip away at the part of yourself that used to flinch. You become calm under pressure. You move with quiet fire. You're no longer relying on mood swings to guide your action. You've replaced emotion with execution.

You're not just a man who *wants* to be better. You're a man who *does* better. Consistently. Silently. Daily. And that's the man who wins.

Master the Rule of 3: Time, Energy & Focus

Let's get this straight: most men aren't failing because they're lazy. They're failing because their attention is fractured, their energy is leaking, and their time is spent reacting instead of building. They're stuck in the noise. They wake up and scroll, jump from one half-task to another, juggle ten browser tabs, check their phone eighty times before lunch, and wonder why they feel burnt out by mid-afternoon without actually accomplishing anything that moves the needle.

It's not about intelligence. It's not about potential. It's about direction. Most men are trying to push a car uphill with the brakes on. They're chasing goals without systems, sprinting without strategy, and constantly running from one thing to the next without clarity on *why* they're doing any of it.

Enter the Rule of 3. This isn't a productivity gimmick. It's a code for men who are done wasting effort on chaos. It's a tool to anchor your time, protect your energy, and direct your focus toward what actually matters. The Rule of 3 means: every day, you choose **three clear, non-negotiable priorities**. Not errands. Not busywork. Not fluff. Just three things that matter — things that, if you executed on them today, you'd move closer to who you want to be. Three. Not five. Not twelve. Not whatever your scattered to-do list tells you. Three.

Why three? Because more than that, and your attention dilutes. Less than that, and you're not challenging yourself. Three forces clarity. It makes you decide what matters *most*

43

today, and then build your day around it. Not the other way around. Most men wake up and *react*. They let their phones, emails, and moods dictate what happens next. But when you apply the Rule of 3, your day begins with *intentional control*. You lead. You don't chase. You don't bounce between tasks. You execute.

The man who gets three important things done per day, every day, is a dangerous man. Because those wins compound. Every day, he's laying bricks. Not just moving dirt. Not just "staying busy." He's building something real.

Discipline Over Chaos: Time, Energy, Focus

We've been told to manage time, but here's the truth: time means nothing without energy and focus. You can schedule twelve hours of productivity on your calendar, but if your brain is fried and you're checking your phone every five minutes, those hours mean nothing. You were present physically but absent mentally — and you can't build anything strong in that state.

Energy is your real currency. Focus is your weapon. And time? Time is just the field they fight on. To master your day, you need to understand this triad: **time, energy, and focus must align**. You want to protect your best hours — your highest-energy zones — and aim your deepest focus at your biggest priorities. You don't schedule your most important task for when you're already mentally gassed. You don't burn your morning clarity on emails and errands. You don't let your attention bleed out on distractions and pretend you're being productive.

The Rule of 3 is about protecting these three resources with ruthless discipline. You start by identifying your *non-negotiable priorities* in the morning. You block out time for them — real time, not "when I get to it." You defend that time like your future depends on it, because it does.

Then, you monitor your energy. You start noticing when you feel sharp, when you're slipping, when your body needs movement or fuel or rest. You stop running your day like a robot. You start running it like a high-performer — someone who understands their limits and optimizes around them.

Focus is where the real battle happens. If you can't hold your focus for more than five minutes, you'll never go deep enough to create anything meaningful. Real progress doesn't come from shallow multitasking. It comes from uninterrupted, sustained effort. That means putting your phone away. That means saying no to digital noise. That means choosing silence over stimulation — and staying in it long enough to *finish* something that matters. Distraction isn't an accident anymore. It's engineered. Every app, every platform, every notification is designed to hijack your brain. You don't "kind of" check your phone — you *train your mind* to stay fractured. And every time you give in, you weaken your ability to lock in.

You want to build the Chad Mindset? Learn to hold focus. Learn to shut out the world. Learn to enter that deep state where your work becomes war — where you don't check the clock, don't switch tasks, don't drift. You just execute. Time. Energy. Focus. When those three align under the Rule of 3, you become a force. You get more done in three hours than most people do in three days. Not because you're a machine. Because you stopped being a slave to chaos.

System > Willpower: Living the Rule

The Rule of 3 only works if it lives in a system — a rhythm that removes guesswork and decision fatigue. You don't want to wake up and "feel out" your priorities. You want to lock in the night before. You don't want to fight for focus. You want to create conditions that protect it. You don't want to rely on motivation. You want structure that *moves you*, no matter how you feel.

Start here: every night, before bed, you write down your three. Three outcomes that matter. Three things that will make tomorrow a win. You do this *before* the day begins, so there's no space for laziness or impulse to hijack your mission. When you wake up, it's already decided. Then, you block time. Your number one task gets your highest energy window. Not when you're tired. Not after scrolling. First. Full focus. No distractions. You sit, you breathe, and you do the work. Nothing else matters in that window. Your second and third priorities fall into place after that, protected by the same system — blocked time, full energy, sharp focus.

This is where most men fail — they try to remember their goals in the middle of a noisy day. They try to "find time." They try to squeeze focus between distractions. You can't win like that. You don't squeeze greatness into a corner. You *build space* for it — and you defend that space like your future depends on it. You need to become a man who others can't reach during his focus hours. Not rude. Just unavailable. You need to be a man who doesn't check his phone during deep work. Who doesn't start the day in reactive mode. Who isn't thrown off course by every buzz, ping, or email.

This is how discipline works. Not in big motivational moments, but in small, daily systems. You sharpen your mind by doing the same thing at the same time, with the same focus, every day — until it becomes automatic. Until it becomes identity. At the end of each day, you review. Did I hit my three? Where did I drift? What blocked me? What needs adjusting? You don't judge. You just observe. You refine. You re-aim. And you show up again — better, cleaner, sharper.

Because that's what separates men who talk from men who *build*. One group waits to feel ready. The other has a system that runs no matter what. Three priorities. One focus at a time. Full energy behind each. That's it. That's the code. That's how you take your mind, your calendar, your life back.

Your Environment Is Lying to You

Take a hard look at your environment — your room, your digital space, your people. Look at your desk. Your bedroom. The tabs on your browser. The apps on your phone. The people you text most. That is your reality. That's the software running in the background of your brain all day long. You may think you're making your own decisions, but the truth is, your environment is shaping most of them before you even realize it.

You don't rise above your environment. You get dragged down by it or pulled forward by it — and most men are being dragged. Your space trains your behavior. If you live in clutter, you think in clutter. If your phone is a dopamine machine, your focus will collapse every time you touch it. If your friends are weak, undisciplined, or negative, your drive will rot from the inside. You can't out-discipline chaos forever. Eventually, your surroundings win. If your physical, digital, and social environments are all misaligned with your goals, then you're fighting a losing battle. You may be motivated. You may be smart. You may even have a great plan. But your surroundings will quietly sabotage you — every day — until the mission dies from exhaustion.

This chapter is your wake-up call: your environment is either lying to you or leading you. It's either reminding you who you are and what you're building — or constantly distracting you, draining you, and numbing your fire. You want mental clarity, focus, and discipline? Start with where you live, what you see, what you hear, and who you allow in your space. Not just once. Every day. Every moment. Because environment isn't background noise. It's the stage your life plays out on — and you've been living on a stage that's been feeding your worst habits, not your best ones.

Cluttered Room, Cluttered Mind, Cluttered Life

Let's start with the physical. Most men are living in low-grade chaos. Their room looks like it belongs to a teenager. Laundry everywhere. Trash on the floor. Screens glowing at 2 AM. A bed that's never made. A desk that hasn't seen the surface in weeks. Empty bottles, snack wrappers, wires, clutter, mess. And somehow, they expect their mind to feel clear. Sharp. Focused. That's not how this works. Your external space bleeds into your internal state. It's not just about cleanliness. It's about *control*. If the space around you is neglected, it trains your brain to accept that standard. Every time you walk into a room that looks like disorder, you're subtly reinforcing the idea that *this is normal*. That comfort, chaos, and laziness are acceptable. That you're not in charge.

But when your room is clean, your bed is made, your space is clear, and everything has a place — your mind shifts. You feel calmer. More intentional. More powerful. It's a signal: I am in control of my space, and therefore, in control of myself.And it's not just about your bedroom. It's your whole physical environment. What's in your fridge? What's on your bathroom sink? What posters are on your wall? What does your closet look like? What do you keep next to your bed? All of it is talking to your subconscious. Constantly. Repeating little phrases like: "you're still a boy," or "you're not serious," or worse — "you've already given up."

You want to break free? Start where you stand. Clean your room like a man who respects himself. Throw out what doesn't serve you. Fold your clothes. Organize your tools. Set up your space for movement, discipline, and focus. Every object you see should either support your goals or get out of your way. Because if you keep living in disorder, don't be surprised when your mind feels heavy. When your decisions feel reactive. When your willpower runs out before the day even begins. This isn't about aesthetics. This is about ownership. Control your space, or it will control you.

Your Feed Is Your Reality — Curate It Like Your Life Depends On It

Now let's talk about your digital environment — the one you carry in your hand every waking hour.

Your phone isn't just a tool anymore. It's your second brain. And for most men, it's poisoned. Open your screen time report and you'll see the truth. Hours lost to Instagram, TikTok, YouTube, messaging, endless loops of short dopamine hits that rewire your attention span into fragments. You're not watching content — you're being programmed by it.

If you let your phone run on autopilot, it will destroy your focus. Slowly. Quietly. Daily. It will replace your ambition with distraction. Your attention with stimulation. Your energy with fatigue. You'll spend your prime hours feeding on other people's content, thoughts, opinions, and lives — and wonder why you feel so lost in your own. Every app you keep is a doorway. Every notification is a hook. Every swipe is a tiny negotiation with your mission. Your phone is either your weapon or your leash — there's no neutral. So here's the move: audit everything.

Delete the apps you don't need. Silence notifications that don't serve your focus. Remove temptation instead of trying to resist it. Rearrange your home screen so it doesn't hijack your brain every time you unlock it. Unfollow accounts that entertain you but don't *elevate* you. Follow people who move the needle. Who teach. Who challenge. Who build. Curate your digital space like it's your command center — because it is.

Then go deeper. Control your tabs. Keep your desktop clean. Unsubscribe from junk email. Close the endless mental loops. Set time limits. Create folders. Make rules. The more friction you remove from distraction, the less mental power you waste fighting yourself.

And most importantly: spend less time consuming, and more time creating. Use your phone to track, train, record, write, build. Use it as a tool for direction — not sedation. The goal isn't to live off the grid. The goal is to live in control. You don't need to be perfect. But you do need to stop pretending your phone is innocent. Because right now, it's winning. And until you fix your digital environment, your discipline will keep leaking out the back door — no matter how hard you work.

You Can't Build a Warrior's Mind Surrounded by Sheep

Let's get brutally honest: your environment also includes your people — and most men don't realize how much their inner circle is sabotaging them. If your closest friends are unmotivated, weak, addicted, pessimistic, undisciplined, or still living like they're 17, that energy *infects* you. You become who you spend time with — not because you copy them consciously, but because your nervous system calibrates to the average of their standards. Every interaction trains your brain to accept a certain level of effort, ambition, focus, and truth.

So ask yourself: who are the five people you spend the most time with? Do they challenge you? Inspire you? Are they strong, direct, moving forward in life? Or are they lost, soft, full of excuses?

Most men are too scared to cut people off. They think loyalty means holding onto relationships that no longer serve them. But here's the truth: you're not responsible for their growth — you're responsible for yours. And if someone's energy pulls you backward, that's not loyalty. That's self-betrayal. This doesn't mean you ghost everyone. It means you *audit access*. You start seeing your time and presence as sacred. You don't entertain nonsense. You don't hang around people who drain you. You don't tolerate energy that slows you down. You create distance. You raise standards. And if they rise with you? Good. If not? You move on. Better to walk alone than in the wrong crowd. Because once your circle shifts, everything else follows. You think clearer. You move faster. You push harder. Your default level of discipline rises — not because you're trying harder, but because the people around you *don't allow weakness*. And that pressure turns you into someone sharper, stronger, and more dangerous than ever before.

Environment is identity. If your room is sharp, your mind sharpens. If your phone is clean, your attention follows. If your people are focused, you rise by proximity. None of this is accidental. You build it. You choose it. And when you do, your entire life becomes aligned with your mission. You stop wondering why you're stuck — and start moving with force.

PART IV: BECOME A CHAD IN THE WORLD – CONFIDENCE & CONNECTION

Social Confidence Is a Skill: Train It Like One

Let's kill the myth right here: confidence is not some innate trait reserved for the loud, the tall, or the extroverted. It's not in your genes. It's not in your jawline. It's not something you "either have or don't." That idea has kept too many men small, silent, and stuck in their heads.

Social confidence is a *skill*. Period. Just like lifting, just like discipline, just like mental toughness. And like any other skill, it's trainable — through action, repetition, and failure. Especially failure. But most guys don't train it. They avoid it. They rationalize their awkwardness with phrases like "I'm just not good with people" or "I'm introverted" or "I overthink it." As if that's permanent. As if that's a life sentence.

It's not. The real problem is this: modern life gives you every excuse to hide. You can text instead of call. You can ghost instead of confront. You can scroll instead of engage. You can live behind a username, a filter, a meme page — and call it connection. But deep down, you know that's not it. That's not how you build presence. That's not how you lead. That's not how you walk into a room and *own it*.

Confidence isn't about being loud. It's about being grounded. It's about walking into a situation and trusting yourself to handle it — without overthinking, without shrinking, without folding. It's the quiet power of knowing that whatever happens, you'll be okay. And that power comes from *exposure* — not from theory. You don't beat social anxiety by reading about it. You beat it by walking into uncomfortable situations again and again until your nervous system catches up with your goals. Until talking to people feels like breathing. Until rejection doesn't even register as pain — just feedback. You build social confidence the same way you build a body: one rep at a time. One awkward moment at a time. One "I'd rather avoid this but I won't" at a time.

And eventually, the reps add up. Your self-talk changes. You stop hesitating. You stop rehearsing imaginary conversations in your head. You show up, speak up, and move forward. Confidence stops being something you chase — and becomes something you *own*.

Talk Like You Belong — Because You Do

Let's get into what confidence actually looks like in conversation. Most guys think it's about having the perfect words, the funniest joke, the smartest take. It's not. It's about energy, intent, and presence.

If you walk into a room with your shoulders slumped, eyes down, breath shallow, and thoughts racing — you're telling everyone (and yourself) that you don't belong. And then you try to "think your way out" of that energy, which only makes you sound more robotic, awkward, and self-conscious.

Presence starts with the body. Stand tall. Breathe deep. Speak slower than you think you should. Make eye contact — not like a stare down, but like you're *there*. Fully there. That alone puts you in the top 10% of men. Because most people are disconnected — from others and from themselves.

Then speak from your chest. Not your throat. Not your head. Your *chest*. Like your words have weight. Like you're not waiting for permission to exist in the room. You don't need to be loud. Just solid. Unapologetic. Centered.

Now, let's talk about what to *say* — because most social anxiety is rooted in a fear of saying the "wrong thing." But that fear is backwards. People don't remember your words. They remember how you made them feel. If you make them feel seen, respected, energized, or challenged, they'll want more of your presence — regardless of how smooth or smart you sounded. Ask real questions. Not surface-level stuff you don't care about. Not robotic lines you read on Reddit. Speak like you're actually curious. Like you actually give a damn. Because you should. Most people are dying to be heard. You want to be magnetic? Listen like you mean it.

And when the moment comes to speak your truth — don't hedge. Don't filter yourself into beige nothingness. Say what you think. Say it calmly, clearly, and without needing approval. If someone disagrees, good. That's not rejection — that's engagement.

Every time you enter a conversation with full presence, open intent, and no apologies — you build confidence. You send your brain a signal: *we can handle this*. And the more you do it, the more natural it becomes. Until one day, you realize you're not "faking" confidence anymore.

You *are* confident. Because you've earned it.

Rejection Is Not a Threat — It's the Rep

Let's talk about rejection — the ghost in every anxious man's head.

You fear rejection not because it hurts, but because you *believe* it means something about your worth. You treat it like a verdict. Like it proves something is wrong with you. That's a lie your brain tells to protect you from discomfort. But in protecting you, it paralyzes you.

Rejection isn't a threat. It's a *rep*. Every "no" is proof that you're doing the work. That you're getting your reps in. That you're building scar tissue in the right places. You don't avoid rejection. You hunt it — like a warrior sharpening his sword.

You're not soft anymore. You're not waiting for the perfect moment, the right mood, the ideal outcome. You're in the field, on the ground, face to face with life. And that includes being turned down, brushed off, misread, or ignored. All of it. Because none of that breaks you. It forges you.

Your confidence doesn't grow when people like you. It grows when they don't — and you stay grounded anyway. When the conversation dies and you don't spiral. When the girl says no and you *smile*. When the joke doesn't land and you own it. That's power. That's presence. That's the mindset of a man who isn't shaped by reactions.

Every socially powerful man you've ever seen got there by getting rejected *more* than you. Not less. They just didn't attach meaning to it. They didn't take it personally. They saw it for what it was: feedback. Noise. A bump in the rep count.

The more rejection you collect, the less it affects you. The fear shrinks. The hesitation dies. The overthinking fades. You stop avoiding. You stop stalling. You start speaking, acting, *leading*. And that's when confidence stops being a performance — and starts becoming part of your nervous system. You're not socially awkward. You're just untrained. You're not afraid of people. You're afraid of *yourself* in front of people. And the only way to fix that? Exposure. Intention. Reps.

Start small. One conversation a day. One compliment. One question. One moment of speaking before you're ready. Do it again tomorrow. And again the next day. Until the fear is gone and the fire is real. That's how you train confidence. That's how you become the man who owns the room — not with noise, but with *presence*.

The Real Modern Masculinity

Look around. The modern man is confused. Half the world tells him to soften up, to be more agreeable, to stay quiet, to apologize for his nature. The other half screams at him to "be alpha," to dominate, to posture, to shout about masculinity like it's a costume you put on for social media. And caught between these two extremes, most men have lost their sense of what it actually means to *be* a man.

Masculinity isn't toxic. Weakness is. Repression is. Pretending to be something you're not — that's what poisons you. Real masculinity doesn't need to shout. It doesn't need to prove. It doesn't need to put others down to feel strong. It's quiet, consistent, directional, grounded. It doesn't compete with men who don't matter or argue with people who don't understand it. It simply *is*.

But most men today were never taught that. They were raised without role models, without initiation, without clear standards for manhood. They were told to be nice, not strong. To fit in, not stand firm. To be "safe," not powerful. They were taught to repress the instinct to lead, to fight, to pursue — and then they were left wondering why they feel aimless, anxious, and invisible.

Masculinity isn't a mask. It's a structure. It's the frame that holds your character upright. When that frame is gone, everything collapses. You get men who drift through life without direction, who crumble under pressure, who avoid conflict at all costs. You get men addicted to comfort, to approval, to validation. You get men who have no idea who they are without someone telling them.

But here's the truth: masculinity was never the enemy. It's the medicine.

Masculinity is *direction* when the world is chaos. It's *composure* when emotion runs wild. It's *duty* when others choose distraction. It's *integrity* when lies are easy. It's *courage* when comfort tempts you to shrink. You don't have to scream "I'm a man" to live those values. You just have to embody them — silently, daily, relentlessly. Because real strength isn't loud. It's stable. It's not flexed in the mirror. It's lived in the small decisions you make when no one's watching.

Honor and Integrity — The Forgotten Code

You want to stand out as a man in this generation? Keep your word.

That's it. That's how low the bar is. Most men today can't follow through on a promise to themselves, let alone to others. They say one thing, do another, and then hide behind excuses or mood swings. But integrity — the ability to align your words, your actions, and your values — is the foundation of masculine power. Without it, you're just noise.

Honor is not an old-fashioned concept. It's the most modern advantage you can have in a world that runs on dishonesty and self-interest. When you're the man who keeps his word, who does what he says he will, who refuses to gossip, who doesn't flinch when truth gets uncomfortable — people feel it. They may not always like you, but they'll trust you. They'll respect you. And most importantly, *you'll respect yourself.*

Honor is living by a code that doesn't bend under pressure. It's not moral posturing. It's discipline. It's showing up to the hard things even when they don't pay off immediately. It's being direct with people instead of pretending. It's saying "no" when everyone else says "yes" to keep peace. It's having hard conversations, not hiding from them. It's telling the truth even when your voice shakes.

That's what separates boys from men — emotional composure under pressure. A man doesn't react to every emotion like a leaf in the wind. He feels deeply, but he doesn't drown in it. He observes. He decides. He acts. The ability to remain calm in conflict, focused in chaos, and centered in criticism is what gives him gravity. People sense it. They lean toward it. That's what makes masculine energy so powerful — it stabilizes the environment around it.

And no, this doesn't mean being cold or emotionless. Emotional control isn't suppression — it's mastery. It's knowing when to express and when to hold. It's being honest about what you feel without letting those feelings steer the ship. A weak man reacts. A strong man responds. That's the difference between being ruled by emotion and being in command of it.

So when you think of masculinity, don't think of dominance or posturing. Think of presence. Think of integrity. Think of a man whose life is aligned from the inside out — who doesn't have to fake confidence or force respect, because his behavior *earns* it every day.

That's the quiet power of modern masculinity. It doesn't demand the spotlight. It creates one.

Strength With Class — The Evolution of the Chad

Let's be honest — the word "masculine" has been hijacked. It's been turned into either a weapon or a meme. You've got the hyper-aggressive "alpha" influencers yelling about conquest, money, and dominance like a broken record, and the passive "nice guys" begging for validation while resenting the world for not noticing their kindness. Both are missing the point.

True masculinity is neither of those. It's not about being a jerk, and it's not about being harmless. It's about being *capable* — and restrained. Dangerous, but disciplined. Strong, but composed. Confident, but humble. It's not about proving you're a man. It's about embodying it.

You don't have to project toughness. You have to *earn* it — through consistent action, through the way you treat people, through the standards you set for yourself. A masculine man doesn't seek to control others. He controls *himself*. He doesn't chase validation. He commands respect through presence. He doesn't fear emotion. He integrates it into purpose. That's strength with class.

Class is what separates power from arrogance. A man with class doesn't need to humiliate others to feel strong. He doesn't flex wealth, status, or dominance to feel seen. He carries his success quietly, confidently, and lets his results speak louder than his mouth. You can feel it when he walks in the room — not because he's loud, but because he's *centered*.

That's the modern Chad — not a caricature of masculinity, but its evolution. A man who's physically strong, mentally sharp, emotionally grounded, and spiritually aligned. A man who can fight but prefers peace. Who can lead but also listen. Who can feel deeply without losing his edge. Who's not trying to be better than other men — just better than the man he was yesterday.

And the world needs more of that. Because chaos needs structure. Weaknesses need leadership. Fear needs direction. The masculine ideal is not outdated — it's endangered. But if you embody it with class, integrity, and composure, you become rare. And in a world addicted to chaos and confusion, rarity is power.

So no more hiding your strength. No more apologizing for being assertive, ambitious, or direct. And no more cosplaying masculinity like it's a performance. Build it quietly. Live it fully. Carry it with class.

Because being a man was never the problem. Forget the noise.
The world doesn't need less masculinity. It needs better men.

Women, Sex & The Chad Code

You've been lied to about women. You've been told to chase, to impress, to "win" them over, to play games and manipulate emotions. You've been told to memorize lines, read signals, and perform like a trained monkey just to get attention. You've been told that confidence means dominance, that attraction is control, and that sex is conquest. None of that is true. That's not confidence — that's insecurity wearing a mask.

Real masculine energy doesn't chase approval. It commands attention by existing fully, by being *rooted* in who you are, by radiating stability in a world full of noise. Women aren't drawn to men who need them. They're drawn to men who *lead themselves*. To men who are calm, clear, directed — who have a mission that doesn't revolve around validation or sex.

You don't attract through performance. You attract through *presence*.

Presence is when you're grounded in your body, when your eyes meet someone else's and you don't flinch or overthink, when your energy isn't scattered by insecurity or need. Presence says, "I'm here, I'm whole, I don't need to prove anything." It's the kind of energy that doesn't demand attention — it draws it in naturally, like gravity.

That's why chasing never works. Because chasing signals lack. It screams that you've placed someone else on a pedestal and yourself beneath them. It makes you forget your own value. When your attention is desperate, your energy becomes weak. You start adapting, pleasing, bending, selling instead of *being*.

Women feel that instantly. Not through words — through instinct. Attraction isn't logic; it's energy. And energy doesn't lie.

The Chad Code starts here: stop chasing. You're not trying to *get* women. You're trying to *become* the kind of man they want to follow — not because you tricked them, but because you earned their respect.

Lead yourself first. Master your mind. Train your body. Build your mission. Fill your life with meaning and momentum. Then bring a woman into that world if she adds to it — not because you need her to complete it. That's masculine power. You're not begging for connection. You're *choosing* it. When you live this way, attraction stops being a game. It becomes alignment.

Sexual Energy: Power, Not Addiction

Let's talk about sex — not the way the internet does, not the way locker rooms do, but the way a man should. Because the way you handle your sexual energy determines your level of focus, creativity, and control.

Most men waste it. They're addicted to stimulation, trapped in loops of porn, fantasies, and empty release. They spend their power chasing dopamine instead of channeling it into purpose. Then they wonder why they feel tired, dull, and unmotivated. You can't spend all day indulging your lowest impulses and expect to feel like a warrior.

Sexual energy is your most potent life force. It's desire in motion — the raw, primal energy that drives creation, risk, ambition, and connection. If you don't direct it consciously, it controls you. You end up restless, unfocused, needing constant novelty to feel alive. That's why discipline around sex and energy isn't about repression — it's about *transmutation.*

Transmutation means taking that same hunger and redirecting it toward creation — your work, your training, your art, your mission. It's learning to live with desire without always needing to discharge it. To feel that fire and use it to build something. To turn lust into momentum. That's what separates a man who's enslaved by his urges from a man who channels them into greatness.

You can still enjoy sex — deeply, passionately, with full presence. But it's no longer your main source of validation or identity. You're not chasing women to prove your worth. You're connecting with women as an *extension* of your worth — as an exchange of energy between two people who respect themselves and each other.

That shift changes everything. Because when a man is ruled by lust, women can feel it. His gaze is hungry. His presence is scattered. He's not there — he's consuming. But when a man has mastered his energy, his presence feels *safe.* Grounded. Powerful. He doesn't chase. He chooses. He doesn't take. He connects. He doesn't need. He invites.

That's what women respond to — not looks, not money, not smooth talk. *Energy.* Controlled power. Masculine calm.

Desire without desperation. A disciplined man is magnetic because he's rare.

The Chad Code: Lead, Respect, Build

Attraction is simple, but it's not easy. The modern man complicates it because he's been taught to fear women or worship them. He's either terrified of rejection or obsessed with approval. He's either cold and defensive or desperate and available. Both extremes are weaknesses.

The Chad Code is balance — self-respect in connection, strength without arrogance, openness without need. You're not trying to "win" a woman. You're showing up as a whole man who's already building, already leading, already fulfilled — and you're inviting her to join your world. Not to fix you, not to complete you, but to *grow with you*.

That's masculine leadership. It's not dominance — it's direction. It's saying, "This is where I'm going," and walking there whether someone follows or not. When you move like that, the right people align with you naturally. You stop needing to convince anyone. You stop fearing rejection. You stop pretending.

Confidence in dating doesn't come from strategy. It comes from *self-trust*. From knowing you'll be fine with or without the outcome. From knowing your standards are clear. From knowing you're not negotiating your identity to earn affection. And that's the ultimate Chad move — you stop negotiating your value. You stop overcompensating, oversharing, or overselling. You stop asking, "What can I say to make her like me?" and start asking, "Does this woman align with my mission, my values, my energy?" That's not arrogance. That's awareness. It's shifting from consumer to creator. From beggar to builder. From boy to man.

Women are not tests. They're reflections. They mirror your energy back to you. If you're grounded, they relax. If you're uncertain, they hesitate. If you're needy, they pull away. When you lead with integrity and purpose, they can feel it. It's not something you say. It's something you *are*.

So here's the truth, stripped of every filter and game: women want men who are *already whole*. Men who don't beg for attention or validation. Men who have their shit together. Men who move with direction, emotional control, and respect. Men who build. Because in the end, Chad doesn't chase. Chad doesn't play games. Chad doesn't perform. **Chad builds — himself, his world, his standards.** And everything worth having is drawn to that.

PART VI: COMMAND YOUR LIFE AND FIND PEACE

Why Discipline Alone Isn't Enough

There comes a point where doing more stops working. You've built discipline. You've built habits. You show up. You train. You journal. You grind. But underneath all the structure, something still feels off — a low hum of restlessness, friction, fatigue. It's not burnout, not quite. It's something subtler: **you're always on**.

And it's killing your edge.

Most men who reach this stage don't slow down — they double down. More checklists. More output. More caffeine. They think they need to optimize harder. But the problem isn't output. It's *orientation*. You're not weak — you're stuck in the wrong mode.

Hustle Mode is what builds your foundation. It's messy, aggressive, unsustainable — and necessary. You need it when you're soft, distracted, undisciplined. Hustle gets you off the couch. It breaks inertia. It pushes you into the arena. But hustle isn't meant to be permanent. It's a launchpad, not a long-term lifestyle. Stay in that gear too long and you hit diminishing returns. Every task becomes frantic. Every decision starts to cost more. You chase ten things and finish none. You move fast but not far. Enter **Command Mode**.

Command Mode is what happens *after* discipline is built. It's not about pushing harder — it's about acting with clarity, calm, and control. You conserve energy, sharpen decisions, and move like a man with nothing to prove. It's not about *doing less*. It's about doing *only what matters*, and doing it with unshakable intent.

The difference is felt instantly. In your tone. In your body. In your posture. You go from anxious action to quiet precision. From chasing to drawing things toward you. From sprinting to *directing*.

This shift isn't motivational. It's neurological. It's psychological. It's strategic. And if you're ready for it, it will change the entire texture of your life.

You don't need more hustle. You need *command*.

The Psychology of Precision: Flow, Fatigue & Control

Let's break down what's actually happening when you live in Hustle Mode for too long.

1. Decision Fatigue - Every choice drains you. What to wear. What to train. What to eat. What to prioritize. When you don't have clear systems or non-negotiables, you spend all day thinking about what you're supposed to be doing — instead of just *doing it*. You feel productive, but you're leaking energy constantly.

Command Mode eliminates this by installing defaults. You don't decide what to do — you follow what's already been decided. Your days become structured around *essentials*, not scattered intentions. Less mental clutter = more sharp execution.

2. Constant Fight-or-Flight - Hustle Mode feels exciting — but it's rooted in stress hormones. Cortisol, adrenaline, urgency. It works — for a while. But long term, it burns you out. You stop sleeping deeply. Your focus shatters. You lose your edge with women, with business, with training. You're tense — not composed.

Command Mode shifts your nervous system into *flow-state training*. You move from reactivity to deliberate calm. Your breathing slows. Your voice lowers. Your attention expands. You start running your life like a black-ops unit, not a caffeinated intern.

3. Disconnection from Results - When you're always doing, you stop evaluating. You stay busy but never stop to ask: *is this actually working?* You lose strategic vision. Hustle becomes a loop. You don't just need to work hard — you need to *adjust*. To review. To recalibrate based on real data.

That's where **Mission Audits** come in. Once a week, you step out of the trenches and ask:

- What did I do this week that moved the mission forward?
- What felt like noise? What drained me?
- What's one adjustment that could simplify my execution next week?

This keeps you sharp. Not reactive. Not emotional. Just clear.

Because Command Mode doesn't mean passive. It means *surgical*. Focused. Clean. You work from *above* the battlefield

— not lost in the fog. And when you live from that place, something shifts. You stop chasing success like a starving dog. You *move differently*. You become the type of man whose presence *precedes* his reputation. This is where real leadership begins.

Installing the Operator: Daily Structure for Command Mode

You don't wait for Command Mode. You *train it*. It starts by rebuilding your day around fewer, deeper priorities — and removing anything that scatters your energy. The structure doesn't need to be perfect. It needs to be *repeatable*. You're not scripting your life minute by minute — you're installing rhythm. Here's a field-tested template to get you started:

Morning Protocol – First 90 Minutes (Zero Input)

No phone. No news. No inbox. The first 90 minutes are yours and yours alone.

- Wake at the same time (even on weekends — rhythm is power).
- 5–10 minutes breathwork or silence. You *arrive* into the day, not rush into it.
- 20–30 minutes training. Doesn't have to be intense. Move your body with intent.
- Mission review. Look at your top 3 outcomes for the day. Visualize them done.

You don't start your day in response mode. You start in *command*.

Work Blocks – 2 to 3 Deep Zones

You don't need to grind 10 hours. You need *two to three deep zones of undistracted effort.*

Each "zone" is 60–90 minutes of total focus. No multitasking. No breaks. No notifications. You enter with a clear objective, and you *leave only when it's done.* Between zones, take real breaks. Walk. Breathe. Reset. You're not a robot — you're a *weapon.* Rest is part of the reload.

Mission Audit – 10 Minutes at Night

Before bed, you *close the loop* on the day.

- What did I accomplish?
- What did I learn?
- How do I feel?
- What's one small thing I can improve tomorrow?

This audit keeps you from drifting. It rewires your brain for execution — not overthinking. You sleep lighter. You wake sharper. This structure isn't restrictive. It's *liberating.* Because Command Mode isn't about rigidity. It's about rhythm. It's about creating an environment where excellence becomes the path of least resistance. Once you build it — your *default* state becomes power.

You don't need more input.
You don't need more dopamine.
You don't need more hustle.
You need *command.*

Why Stillness Matters (Now More Than Ever)

We live in a state of constant noise — digital alerts, information overload, societal pressure, economic stress, overstimulation. Most men today aren't suffering from weakness — they're suffering from *internal chaos*. Minds that don't shut off. Emotions that spike and spiral. Bodies that never fully relax.

If you don't build inner stillness, you *stay reactive*. And reactive men are weak men — not because they aren't strong, but because their strength is scattered.

Stillness isn't about being passive or soft. It's about *being in control when it counts*. When your emotions surge, when life gets loud, when people are losing their heads — your edge is the ability to stay composed, focused, and intentional.

This is especially true for the modern man aged 20–35. You're juggling pressure to perform, to look good, to earn more, to stay connected, and to "be someone." But few are teaching you how to hold your center through it all. That's what this chapter is for: not to make you calm — but to make you *clear*, focused, and unshakable in a storm. Let's build it.

What Stillness Actually Is

Stillness isn't about silence or inactivity. It's not sitting in a cave, meditating for hours. Stillness is the *absence of internal noise*. It's mental and emotional *clarity under stress*. It's the ability to stay present and respond instead of react. It's the opposite of being scattered, impulsive, or mentally overclocked.

You've seen it.
The soldier under fire who slows his breath and clears the room. The athlete at the free-throw line with the world watching — locked in. The father staying calm during a family crisis. The leader who doesn't raise his voice but commands the room.

Stillness is practiced. Not gifted.

It's built from three things:

1. **Awareness** — Noticing your internal state in real time.
2. **Regulation** — Having tools to reset your system under pressure.
3. **Intentional Action** — Moving from clarity, not compulsion.

The Chaos We're Up Against

Let's name the threats to your inner peace:

- **Constant Dopamine Spikes** (social media, porn, notifications)
- **Information Fatigue** (news cycles, opinions, algorithm overload)
- **Decision Overload** (career, relationships, identity pressure)
- **Lack of Mental Space** (no time for solitude, always consuming)

This creates a baseline of anxiety and mental clutter. And if you don't learn how to shut that down — you burn out, lash out, or check out. The solution isn't to escape. It's to *equip yourself* with tools to stay still in the storm.

The Science of Stillness: What Actually Works

Here's what's been proven to help build stillness — not hypothetically, but biologically.

1. Controlled Breathing (Combat Breathing / Box Breathing)

Used by military, special ops, and first responders to calm the nervous system under extreme stress. **How to do it:**

- Inhale for 4 seconds
- Hold for 4 seconds
- Exhale for 4 seconds
- Hold for 4 seconds
  Repeat for 1–2 minutes.

This regulates your autonomic nervous system, lowers cortisol (stress hormone), and improves focus and heart rate variability. According to research from Stanford's Huberman Lab, even a single deep breath can begin to downshift your stress response. **Use this:** Before a tough meeting, conversation, workout, or when you feel overwhelmed.

2. Low-Stimulation Mornings

Avoid input for the first 30–60 minutes after waking. No phone. No news. No screens. This is proven to reduce stress and improve dopamine regulation throughout the day. Morning overstimulation destroys your stillness before the day even starts. **What to do instead:**

- Sit in silence for 10 minutes
- Breathe slowly
- Journal 1–2 lines: "What matters today?"
- Move your body lightly (walk, stretch, bodyweight)

These actions signal to your nervous system: *I'm in control.* That tone carries into the rest of your day.

3. Focused Attention Training (Meditation Without the Fluff)

Forget the spiritual jargon. Meditation is simply attention control. In a world hijacking your focus, training it daily is like sharpening your sword. **Simple method (10 minutes):**

- Sit still. Eyes open or closed.
- Focus on the sensation of breathing.
- When thoughts arise, notice — then return to the breath.
- Don't chase thoughts. Don't judge them. Just reset.

Studies from Harvard and UCLA have shown that just 10 minutes of focused meditation per day improves emotional regulation, working memory, and stress tolerance — all core to stillness.

If you hate sitting still? Good. That's the work. That's where the growth is.

4. Environmental Stillness

If your space is chaotic, your mind will be too. External clutter feeds internal noise.

Quick mission audit:

- Is your desk clear or chaotic?
- Is your phone full of junk apps?
- Do you have physical space for silence, reading, thinking?

Stillness is easier when your environment isn't overstimulating you every second. Design your space for focus — or pay the price in anxiety.

Daily Stillness Protocol (Simple Structure)

Here's a real structure to train stillness — without needing hours of free time:

Morning

- Wake up at the same time (consistency reduces anxiety).
- Zero phone for first 30 minutes.
- Sit in silence for 5–10 mins (use breath or journal if needed).
- Move your body — walking or strength.
- Ask yourself: "What are my 1–2 non-negotiables today?"

Midday Reset

- After your first 3–4 hours of work, take 5 minutes.

- Leave the phone. Step outside or sit quietly.
- Practice 1–2 minutes of combat breathing.
- Stretch. Reconnect with your mission. Don't check messages.

Night

- Last hour: no blue light or stimulation.
- Write down: "What drained me today? What restored me?"
- Spend 10 minutes reading or breathing.
- Sleep with intention — not exhaustion.

Do this for 30 days. You will feel calmer, sharper, and more grounded than 99% of men your age.

Real-World Examples of Stillness

◆ Marcus Aurelius (Stoic Emperor)

Ran an empire, wrote *Meditations*, and led through plague and war. His key? Daily reflection and internal control. "You have power over your mind — not outside events. Realize this, and you will find strength."

◆ David Goggins (Modern Discipline Icon)

Stillness in motion. Goggins doesn't just scream — he *sits with pain*. He trains his mind to stay calm under extreme stress. Watch his interviews. Between the intensity is a man who knows how to be still with suffering — and convert it to strength.

◆ Naval Ravikant (Entrepreneur / Philosopher)

Built wealth — then turned to silence. "A calm mind, a fit body, and a house full of love. These things cannot be bought — they must be earned." His stillness isn't spiritual — it's strategic. His productivity comes from how calm his mind is.

Lead Without Needing to Be Liked

Most men want to lead. They want to speak with weight, take charge, walk into a room and command respect. But when it comes time to assert authority, make hard decisions, or say what needs to be said — they flinch. They soften their tone. They hedge their opinions. They try to sound agreeable. Why? Because deep down, they want to be liked.

This is the invisible leash on most young men. The need for approval. It's not just social — it's psychological. You've been conditioned to believe that likability equals success. Blend in, don't upset anyone, smile more, be easy to work with, don't be too intense. That mindset might keep people comfortable — but it will kill your leadership.

Here's the truth: **you can either lead, or you can seek approval — but you can't do both**.

Leadership requires clarity, decisiveness, and a willingness to upset people. If you're afraid to be disliked, you will compromise your standards. You'll say yes when you should say no. You'll tolerate weak behavior in your team. You'll sugarcoat feedback. You'll hold back ideas. You'll shrink. And people can feel it.

Even if you look the part, even if you speak confidently — if your energy is approval-seeking, people won't trust your authority. They'll sense hesitation. They'll feel the neediness behind your words.

What they want — and what earns their respect — is a man who leads with *conviction*, not insecurity. The world is full of "nice guys" who get walked over because they're terrified of disapproval. They mistake agreeableness for leadership. But leadership isn't about pleasing people — it's about protecting standards, making hard calls, and guiding others through discomfort.

The best leaders are not the most liked. They're the most trusted. And trust is built through **consistency, decisiveness, and backbone** — not likability.

Section II: How Real Leaders Think, Speak, and Move

If you want to lead without needing to be liked, you need to retrain how you show up — in how you think, speak, and carry yourself.

Let's break it down.

1. Respect ≠ Approval

One of the biggest mindset shifts you need to make is this: respect is earned through strength and clarity, not charm. Look at great military leaders. Think of **General James Mattis**, known as the "Warrior Monk." Stoic, serious, strategic. He wasn't trying to make people like him — he was making decisions under pressure. And because of that, his troops *respected* him — even when they disagreed.

Or take **Steve Jobs**. Famously intense, blunt, not warm and fuzzy — but his vision and decisiveness inspired fierce loyalty. His team didn't love everything about him. But they followed him because they believed in his mission. You're not trying to be universally liked. You're trying to be **a clear, grounded force that people trust to lead the way**.

2. Authority Without Arrogance

A mistake some men make when rejecting approval-seeking is swinging to the other extreme — becoming aggressive, loud, or condescending. That's not real leadership. That's insecurity in another form.

True authority is quiet. Calm. Measured. It's not about dominating — it's about anchoring. People feel safer around men who are firm but composed. Watch interviews with **Denzel Washington**. Rarely raises his voice. Doesn't overshare. Doesn't try to entertain. But when he speaks, everyone listens. That's *command presence* — not from arrogance, but from emotional control and earned confidence.

3. Speaking Like a Leader

Your language should reflect your mindset. When you lead, your speech must be:

- **Decisive**, not tentative
- **Grounded**, not reactive
- **Clear**, not bloated with justification

Avoid filler language like "I just think..." or "Maybe we could..." or "Does that make sense?" It weakens your position.Speak in terms of *direction*, not explanation. Example:

✗ "I was wondering if maybe we should shift the timeline?"

☑ "The ti meline shifts next week. I'll handle the transition."

Leadership communication is about ownership. You speak in a way that people can follow.

Practical Leadership Drills for Everyday Life

You don't learn leadership by reading. You learn it by doing — repeatedly, under pressure. Here are actionable drills to build your leadership edge and kill the approval habit.

▒ Drill 1: Command Room Presence

Purpose: Train your nonverbal authority and presence without saying a word.

How to do it:

- Walk into a room (work meeting, gym, social space) and deliberately avoid shrinking or rushing.
- Hold eye contact for half a second longer than usual.
- Keep your shoulders back, chin neutral, hands relaxed.
- Don't look for approval — *observe* the room calmly.
- Practice being present without performing.

Why it works: People respond to the *energy* you carry before you speak. Calm confidence is more commanding than fake hype. This drill helps rewire your body language for leadership.

❦ Drill 2: Decisive Speech Reps

Purpose: Build clear, direct communication under pressure.

How to do it:

- Set a timer for 10 minutes. Record yourself answering these prompts:

    1. "Here's what I believe..."
    2. "Here's what needs to happen..."
    3. "Here's where I stand..."

- No hedging. No soft language. Just clarity.
- Rewatch and note any filler phrases, vocal tics, or apologies.
- Repeat weekly.

Why it works: Leadership is about verbal clarity under pressure. This drill forces you to strip fluff from your communication and speak from a grounded place.

◐ Drill 3: Conflict Composure Practice

Purpose: Stay calm and composed in disagreement without retreating or escalating. **How to do it:**

- In conversation, when someone disagrees, *pause* before responding.
- Use a neutral phrase to reset: "I hear you." Or "Got it."
- Then respond with clarity, not emotion.
- Practice detachment from being *liked* — focus on being *clear* and *respected*.

You can train this with a friend: take turns roleplaying arguments or high-stakes conversations. Your goal is to stay calm, centered, and on message. **Why it works**: The ability to hold your center in tension is the backbone of leadership. This drill hardens that skill in real-time.

Final Word: Lead Like a Man, Not a Performer

Men who need to be liked cannot lead. They hesitate. They shrink. They perform. But leadership requires decisions — hard ones. It requires clarity — even when it's unpopular. And it requires presence — even when you're doubted.

Leadership doesn't mean barking orders or pretending to be alpha. It means you:

- Say what others won't say
- Do what others avoid
- Stand where others fall
- Own the outcome, always

The men who rise are the ones who can walk into a room and own it without needing applause. They lead not with noise, but with *certainty*.

And that kind of presence — grounded, firm, composed — is rare. But you can build it. Day by day. Rep by rep. By choosing respect over approval. Command over comfort. Truth over people-pleasing. You weren't born a leader. You become one — the moment you stop asking permission.

The Art of Controlled Aggression

Aggression isn't your enemy. It's your engine. But that engine? Most men never learn how to drive it. So it either stalls out — or it crashes. Aggression is not violence. It's not rage. It's not lashing out. It's raw masculine energy. The internal fuel of progress. The forward force. The push. The drive to break through obstacles, to move toward what matters, to claim space and make something real. It's the current that built empires, defends families, forges leaders, and carries the man who refuses to quit. Every man is born with this energy, but many grow up being taught to fear it.

Told to quiet down, to be agreeable, to be soft. If he's intense, he's called toxic. If he competes, he's punished. So, he represses the fire, smiles through his teeth, and tries to play nice with a world that doesn't reward nice — it respects power. Suppressed aggression doesn't disappear. It leaks. It turns into low-level anxiety, hidden resentment, addiction, or a life that just feels... stuck. You feel the fire but don't know where to put it. You chase distraction, act out in moments of stress, or numb yourself with comfort. And eventually you forget that the fire was ever meant to *build* something.

Aggression isn't dangerous. *Untrained* aggression is. Because aggression is just energy. What you do with it determines whether it builds or burns. And this chapter isn't about killing that energy. It's about turning it into a weapon — sharp, focused, disciplined. Aggression, when controlled, is the most valuable masculine trait a man can develop. It's drive. It's initiative. It's the unwillingness to back down.

And when a man knows how to stay grounded while carrying that fire, he becomes unshakable.

The Biology of Fire — And How to Breathe Through It

Here's what most men don't understand: you're supposed to be aggressive. It's written into your biology. Testosterone fuels your drive, assertiveness, and competitive edge. It's not just about sex or muscle. It's the hormone that pushes you forward, helps you take risks, assert yourself, and pursue challenges. When it's low, you feel flat. When it's balanced, you feel ready. And aggression is one of the purest expressions of it. But the key is *how* you express it. According to research published in the journal *Psychoneuroendocrinology*, testosterone paired with high cortisol — your primary stress hormone — leads to reactive aggression. This is the kind of aggression that blows up under pressure, lashes out in traffic, or ruins relationships. But testosterone paired with low cortisol — meaning you stay calm even under stress — produces assertive, focused, *strategic* aggression. In other words, aggression becomes powerful when it's paired with *composure*. This is why combat athletes train for control. They don't just throw punches. They learn how to breathe under pressure. How to read the room.

How to decide, not just react. The best fighters don't yell — they *watch*. They strike when it counts. Their aggression is always ready, but never wasted. That's the goal. Controlled aggression isn't about being angry. It's about being ready. Most men are either too soft or too chaotic. Controlled aggression is the middle path. You're not passive, and you're not unhinged. You're focused. You're intense. But you're *measured*. Look at how this plays out in daily life. In training — aggression gets you through the last rep, the heavy set, the cold shower, the miles when your legs want to quit. You're not thinking — you're moving. But you're not out of control. You're direct. In business — aggression shows up in your standards. The way you speak with clarity. The way you negotiate, lead meetings, or refuse mediocrity. Aggression becomes your fuel to create, to solve, to dominate your space — not with ego, but with urgency. In conflict — aggression gives you the edge to stand your ground without flinching. It's not about yelling. It's about being the man who doesn't fold under pressure. Who doesn't walk on eggshells. Who can look someone in the eye and say what needs to be said. In creation — aggression is the fire behind your discipline.

The focused tension that says, "I will finish this, no matter what it takes." It's the daily hammer that builds your craft, your brand, your purpose. And when it's time to protect — aggression doesn't hesitate. If your woman is being disrespected, if your mission is under attack, if your standard is being violated — you don't ask for permission. You act. Cleanly. Without apology.

Real Men Don't Suppress Fire — They Shape It

The problem is that most men don't know *where* to put this energy. So they end up suppressing it — and feeling dead inside — or misfiring it — and causing damage. The solution is simple, but not easy: you need an outlet that trains aggression *with control.* Combat sports are the gold standard. Boxing. Jiu-jitsu. Muay Thai. Wrestling. You're in high stress, with stakes, with feedback, and with rules. It's you versus another man. You can't hide behind words. You have to breathe. You have to manage fear. You have to stay calm while moving fast. That's where the fire gets trained. If that's not your thing, find a discipline that activates the same nervous system pathways: heavy lifting, public speaking, cold exposure, intense sales — something that makes your hands shake and forces you to get sharp anyway.

The point isn't violence: violence is never the answer. It's *voluntary discomfort under pressure.* When you do that often enough, you stop fearing your own intensity. You stop overreacting.

You start moving like a man who knows what he's capable of — and doesn't need to prove it. But aggression isn't just for breaking things — it's for *building* them. Building a business is aggression. You're forcing something into existence that didn't exist before. Building a strong body is aggression. You're tearing muscle and rebuilding it. Building a legacy is aggression. You're saying "this is mine — and I'm making it real." If you're constantly tired, distracted, or numb — your aggression has nowhere to go. You don't need more motivation. You need direction. You need targets.

You need to feel your edge again. Controlled aggression doesn't mean you're calm all the time. It means you choose when to unleash. You learn how to bring up the fire and how to cool it down. You learn how to breathe inside chaos.

You learn how to make hard calls without flinching. And when you walk into a room, people *feel* something. Not because you're loud — but because your energy is sharp, clear, and steady. That's the power of a man who owns his edge. Masculine aggression is not something to fear, cancel, or suppress. It's a necessary tool. One that builds. One that protects. One that can carry you farther than motivation ever will. The key is to master it — not numb it, not fear it, not fake it. If you do that, you stop being a danger to yourself. You become a threat to mediocrity. And in a world addicted to softness, that's the edge most men need.

The Quiet Apex: Living Above the Noise

There comes a point where the need to prove dies. Where ambition sharpens into precision. Where noise becomes background, and the man stands still — not because he's lost his fire, but because he finally knows where to direct it.

This is the Quiet Apex. It's not a performance. It's not a brand. It's not a status you post or talk about. It's a way of moving. Of thinking. Of *being*. You've done the work. You've fought through distraction, rejection, chaos, and resistance. You've built the body, sharpened the mind, reclaimed your space, trained your aggression, and stepped into responsibility. And now you face the last challenge — letting go of the need to be seen doing it. Most men never get here.

They get stuck in the loop — chasing validation, upgrading image, collecting wins to impress people they don't even respect. They confuse noise for power. But noise is cheap. Anyone can be loud. Very few can be *calm*. And fewer still can stay calm while being powerful.

That's what this chapter is about. Not more. Less. Not louder. Quieter. Not bigger. *Clearer.* This is the final form of The Chad Mindset — not the guy yelling in the gym, or flexing in every room, but the one who walks into chaos and doesn't flinch.

The man who could dominate but doesn't need to. Who could crush but chooses clarity. Not because he's soft — but because he's complete.

Detachment is Precision

The Quiet Apex Male doesn't talk about mastery. He lives it. He doesn't chase arguments. He controls environments. He doesn't demand attention. He *commands* it — through presence, through action, through consistency. This kind of man is rare. Because it takes a long time to kill the internal noise. We've talked about the distractions — dopamine loops, digital overstimulation, weak environments.

But the deepest noise is internal: the comparison addiction, the need to be liked, the fear of being forgotten. That's the real war. And the final edge is when you step beyond all of that. When peace stops feeling like laziness. When stillness stops feeling like weakness. When silence becomes your power. Detachment is not disinterest. It's not apathy. It's precision. It's knowing what matters and refusing to feed anything else. It's deleting the app, not to punish yourself, but because your focus is worth more.

It's walking away from petty arguments, not because you're avoiding conflict, but because the game is beneath you. It's training with intensity but not talking about it. It's leading without announcing it. It's being deeply rooted — so deeply that no storm can shake you. And here's the twist: most people won't notice.

They'll still look for noise. They'll still respond to flash, to drama, to cheap wins. But you'll know. You'll feel it when you wake up clear and heavy. You'll feel it in your breath, in your walk, in your grip, in your conversations. You'll feel it when you say less and people listen more. That's the apex. The top of the mountain. The edge beyond ego.

Nothing Left to Prove: Just a Life to Live

And what happens when you get there? You *keep moving*. Quietly. Intentionally. Not chasing peaks, but living in rhythm. You go from proving to refining. From grinding to flowing. From reacting to *choosing*. You become dangerous without effort. Useful without pride. Respected without explanation.

The mission never ends. But how you *move* through it changes. You become lighter. Cleaner. More surgical. Your words hit harder because you use fewer. Your days feel fuller because you cut the unnecessary. You know your values, your vision, your code — and that's enough. There's a beauty in this form of life. It's not loud, but it's deep. You train because it centers you. You build because it aligns with you. You lead because it serves something greater than your own ego. You protect because it's your role, not your flex. You speak less, but when you do, it matters.

This is the kind of man women feel safe around, men respect instinctively, and enemies think twice about crossing. Not because he brags — but because he *knows*. You feel it in his eyes. In his posture. In his discipline. And that's the full circle. From weak and reactive to forged and focused. From scattered to still. From noise to presence. From wanting the world to see you — to building a life so real, you don't care if they do.

This is where the Chad Mindset ends — not with applause, but with silence. Not in dominance, but in depth. The real ones know. And they'll feel it when you walk into a room without saying a word. You don't need to be liked. You

don't need to be seen. You just need to keep showing up —
sharp, rooted, useful. No hunger for validation. No chaos
inside. Just calm. Just power. Just the quiet apex. You've
earned it.

PART VI: THE MISSION NEVER ENDS – PURPOSE & LEGACY

Build Your Brotherhood

There's a lie that modern men love to tell themselves — that strength means isolation. That independence means doing everything alone. That if you need people, you're weak. It's the "lone wolf" myth: the image of the hardened, self-made man who fights the world by himself and wins through sheer will. It looks romantic in movies. It sounds noble in quotes. But in reality? Lone wolves don't conquer — they collapse.

The truth is simple: no man thrives alone. No man sharpens himself in a vacuum. No man sustains discipline without accountability or direction without reflection. Even the strongest soldier needs a unit. Even the most disciplined athlete needs a coach, a rival, a team. Without that, your edge dulls. Your fire fades. Your purpose drifts.

Isolation isn't strength — it's slow decay. You start out saying "I don't need anyone," but what you really mean is "I don't trust anyone." And that mistrust hardens into pride, and that pride becomes your cage. You keep your struggles quiet, you hide your doubts, and you slowly sink under the weight of your own silence. You stop being challenged. You stop being seen. You stop being *tested*.

And when a man stops being tested, he starts dying — mentally, emotionally, spiritually.

Brotherhood isn't about dependency. It's about *alignment*. It's about surrounding yourself with men who hold you to a standard, who call you out when you drift, who push you forward when you stall, who remind you of your mission when you start to forget. Brotherhood is iron sharpening iron. It's not comfort. It's friction. It's the kind of honesty that stings but saves you.

Every great man had a tribe. Marcus Aurelius had his Stoics. Alexander had his generals. Every movement, every empire, every legacy worth studying was built by *men who trusted each other enough to go to war together*. Not just literal war — but the daily war of becoming better men.

You don't need hundreds. You need a few — strong, honest, driven, loyal. Men who are not intimidated by your growth but *invested* in it. Men who don't just hype you up when you win but challenge you when you get lazy. That's a real brotherhood. That's what keeps your mission alive when motivation fades.

How Brotherhood Sharpens the Blade

Being part of a tribe doesn't make you weaker. It makes you dangerous — in the best way. It multiplies your force, expands your perspective, and keeps your discipline sharp when life tries to dull it.

When you're alone too long, your ego takes the wheel. You start thinking you're right all the time. You start mistaking comfort for peace. You start letting small habits slide because no one's watching. You stop training as hard. You skip one morning, then two. You justify it. You soften.

Slowly. Quietly. And by the time you notice, you've lost your edge.

That's why men need other men. Brotherhood keeps your ego in check. It reminds you that you're not as strong, as disciplined, or as smart as you think you are — and that's a *good* thing. Because humility is the gate to growth. A real brother won't let you bullshit yourself. He'll look you in the eye and say, "You're slipping." And instead of getting defensive, you'll feel gratitude — because he's protecting your standard.

There's also power in momentum. When you're surrounded by men who are moving, you move faster. Their energy fuels yours. Their progress reminds you what's possible. Their wins push you, their losses humble you, their consistency shames your excuses. That's the magic of collective growth — one man's discipline creates gravity for the others.

And it's not just about motivation. It's about trust. You learn to open up — not in a soft, performative way, but in a way that builds connection. You share your goals, your failures, your challenges. You give and receive feedback without ego. You hold each other accountable — not with judgment, but with respect. That shared vulnerability doesn't weaken you. It forges loyalty. You stop feeling like you're fighting alone, and that gives your mission endurance.

But understand this: not every group of men is a brotherhood. Most are just drinking circles or trauma-sharing clubs. Brotherhood is built on *shared values* — not shared misery. It's not about complaining. It's about *building*.

It's about helping each other rise. You're not there to vent endlessly about how the world is unfair. You're there to build the kind of men who can face that world and *win*. So, choose carefully. Surround yourself with men who are going somewhere. Men who take care of their bodies, their word, their mission. Men who live with direction. You'll know you've found them because you'll feel it — their presence will sharpen yours. That's the feeling of iron against iron.

Find Your Tribe, or Build It

Some men are lucky — they stumble into a good circle naturally. But most have to build it. And that's okay. Brotherhood isn't found by accident. It's *forged*. You start by living by example. You hold your standards high — and you stay consistent. You don't wait for people to inspire you. You *become* the kind of man that disciplined, mission-driven people want to be around. You attract your tribe by walking your talk, not preaching it.

Put yourself where strong men gather — the gym, the mats, creative spaces, business groups, community projects, mentorship circles. Observe. Watch how men carry themselves. You'll know who's real and who's pretending. The real ones don't brag about work ethic — they *embody* it. They don't talk about honor — they *live* it. When you meet men like that, keep them close. Invest in the relationship. Give value. Show loyalty before you expect it.

And if you can't find them? Build them. Create your own circle. Start small. Two or three men with shared principles. Set rules. No gossip. No weakness-glorifying talk. No fake support. Just raw accountability and real growth. Meet regularly. Train together. Read together. Work on goals together. Share wins and failures. Push each other harder than comfort allows. Over time, that small circle becomes your foundation — your council, your forge, your mirror. The place where you stay grounded, where your excuses die, where your standards rise. The world outside may not get it, but you will. Because once you've tasted that kind of brotherhood — real, loyal, growth-focused connection — you'll never want to go back to being a lone wolf again.

Because the lone wolf is not strong — he's starving. The pack is what keeps him alive, sharp, and dangerous. The pack is what reminds him of who he is when the fight gets long. A brotherhood doesn't just make you better. It keeps you from breaking. And when your tribe rises — you rise with it.

Live to Win: Crafting Your 5-Year Mission Plan

Most men drift through life like they've got endless time. They live reactive lives — not built, but improvised. Wake up, go to work, scroll, train a little, maybe chase a hobby, and then collapse into bed with that quiet whisper of "I'll figure it out later."But later never comes. Because drifting doesn't build momentum — it kills it.

You think you're buying yourself time, but what you're really doing is burning it. Every day you float, every week you "plan to start soon," every month you convince yourself that you're just "not ready yet" — that's your mission dissolving right in front of you. No one ever "figures it out" by accident. You decide who you're going to be — and then you *build* it, day by day, decision by decision.

Life isn't random. It's engineered — by someone. If you don't engineer it, someone else will. Your boss, your girlfriend, the algorithm, the system. You'll become part of someone else's plan instead of the author of your own. And that's not living — that's existing with a pulse and no purpose.

Purpose isn't something you stumble upon like treasure in the woods. It's something you *forge*. Through reflection. Through action. Through pain and persistence. It's not given to you — it's revealed to you as you build.

And the only way to build it is to start treating your life like what it is: a campaign. Not a to-do list. Not a checklist of goals you half-finish. A long-term campaign — strategic, relentless, and alive. Every campaign needs a mission, a map, a timeline, and a commander who never quits when things get messy. You are that commander. And your mission? The man you want to become five years from now.

Five years — that's not forever. But it's enough to transform everything about you if you live with focus. You can build a body that commands respect. You can master a craft. You can create financial freedom. You can become a man of composure, influence, and clarity. But only if you stop improvising and start *designing*. You've done enough "winging   it."
Now it's time to *plan it*.

The Blueprint of a Builder

You start with vision. Not vague dreams, not wishful affirmations — a concrete, visceral vision. Picture the man you want to be in five years. Not in fantasy, but in detail. The version of you who lived every day on mission — who followed through, who led, who built. What does his world look like? How does he move? Who does he spend time with? What problems has he solved? What impact does he leave behind? Write it down. Don't just think it. *See it*. If your goals live only in your head, they'll die there too. This is the anchor point of your mission plan — the north star that keeps you from drifting. But vision alone is nothing without a map. So you reverse-engineer it. You take that image and break it into milestones — yearly, monthly, weekly.

You ask: what must be true a year from now for me to be on track? Then, what must happen in the next 90 days to make that possible? Then, what can I do this week to move the needle?

That's how you turn dreams into direction. You shrink the impossible into the actionable. Every massive shift in your life begins as one small, clear task executed with consistency. Don't overcomplicate it. Focus on systems, not outcomes. You can't control the whole campaign at once, but you can control the next mission. You can control the workout, the page, the dollar, the phone call, the journal entry. You win the day, then the week, then the quarter — until one day, you wake up five years later and you're *him*.

But here's the hard truth: the blueprint won't survive contact with chaos unless you anchor it. That's where discipline meets documentation. You track. You review. You journal like a strategist, not a poet. Each night, you record three things: what went right, what went wrong, and what must improve tomorrow. This isn't therapy — it's data. You're studying your habits like a scientist studying results.

Over time, those small reflections create self-awareness — and awareness creates power. You start to see patterns: where you waste time, where you lose focus, where you excel. And once you see it, you can fix it. You stop repeating your failures and start refining your systems. That's how long-term consistency is built — not through hype, but through honest review.

Every empire needs architecture. Every man who wants to lead his own life needs a plan that exists outside of his emotions. Because moods change. Purpose doesn't.

So build the blueprint. Make it physical. Print it. Write it. Review it weekly. Keep it where you can't ignore it. Because if you can see your mission every day, it will start shaping you from the inside out. The blueprint is how you stop being reactive and start becoming inevitable.

Stay the Course When the World Burns

The mission won't go smoothly. It never does. Life will throw distractions, losses, doubts, betrayals, and fatigue at you — not because the universe is cruel, but because it's testing if you're serious. The mission demands resistance. That's what forges the kind of man who can carry it.

You'll have weeks when everything hits the bills, stress, loneliness, fatigue. You'll question if you're built for it. You'll want to run back to comfort, to routine, to numbness. But those moments are the fire. That's when you double down on your systems, not your feelings.

When chaos hits, the untrained man panics. The trained man executes. He opens his plan, checks his bearings, and focuses on the next actionable move. That's how you stay on course. You don't fix everything. You fix the next thing. The key is to keep momentum — no matter how small. Even 60% effort on your worst days beats perfection that never happens. Discipline doesn't mean you feel great every day — it means you *move anyway*.

And you will lose focus at times. You will fail, skip, forget. That's part of it. The difference between the average man and the disciplined one isn't perfection — it's recovery speed. The mission-minded man doesn't spiral. He recalibrates. He adapts. He learns, adjusts, and gets back in motion. Because he knows five years from now, none of these temporary dips will matter — only that he never quit. Remember: purpose doesn't eliminate chaos. It gives it meaning. When you're anchored in a mission bigger than your moods, the noise of the world stops pulling you apart. You become consistent not because life is easy, but because you've chosen direction over distraction.

And if you stay in the fight long enough — if you keep journaling, refining, building, adjusting — one day you'll look back and realize you've crossed the map. The vision you once wrote as fiction is now your reality. The man you used to imagine is the one in the mirror.

Because you didn't wait to "find yourself." You *built* yourself.

You lived like a commander, not a passenger. You executed through storms. You built systems stronger than your emotions. And you never stopped pushing toward the five-year line — no matter how many times the plan changed.

That's what living to win means. It's not about glory or comfort or even success. It's about direction. About ownership. About turning your life into something *intentional.* Five years from now, you'll be someone. The question is — who? Write it. Plan it. Build it. Then live it with the discipline of a man who refuses to drift. Because you weren't born to survive the years ahead. You were built to *win* them. And the man who lives to win never stops expanding the mission.

FINAL SECTION: TOOLS, CHALLENGES & TACTICS

The 30-Day Chad Challenge

As we said, most guys wait for motivation. They wait for the "perfect time," the "right mindset," or for life to calm down. It never does. Life doesn't hand you transformation — it hands you pressure. And if you don't choose your own struggle, life will choose one for you. That's where the 30-Day Chad Challenge comes in.

This isn't a gimmick. It's not about looking good for Instagram or checking boxes. This is about going to war with every part of yourself that's been holding you back — the excuses, the soft habits, the scattered energy, the mental noise. If you've ever told yourself, "I know I'm capable of more," then you're not wrong — but nothing changes until you build a system and step into it with urgency.

Thirty days is short enough to stay focused, but long enough to break cycles. Neuroscience shows that behavior changes take root when they're repeated with intention over time — especially in tight windows of consistency. A study out of

University College London found that the average time to form a new habit is about 66 days, but what matters most isn't the number — it's momentum. Thirty days of aligned action gives you exactly that: momentum.

What's the difference between a man with momentum and one without? Everything. The man with momentum wakes up with direction. He doesn't scroll first thing in the morning. He doesn't wait to "feel ready." He moves, and his action feeds his clarity. The man without momentum overthinks everything. His habits are random. He questions himself, negotiates with comfort, and drowns in micro-decisions.

The Challenge builds momentum through structure. Every single day, you'll hit four core domains — Mental, Physical, Social, and Discipline. These aren't random. They're the pillars of masculine strength. You train these daily, and you start to feel like a man who's actually in command of his life. That confidence doesn't come from positive affirmations — it comes from evidence. And this Challenge is how you build it.

Rules of Engagement — The Mindset You Need Before Day 1

Before you even start Day 1, you need to understand something: this Challenge won't change your life. *You will.* This isn't magic. It's not going to fix your childhood or hand you a million-dollar business. It's a mirror. And what you see in it will reflect exactly what you put in.

So here are the ground rules. First: full ownership. No one is responsible for your execution but you. If you miss a day, no excuses. If you feel tired, no excuses. If you're "too busy," *no excuses*. You want change? Then own every part of the process. No one is coming to rescue you. That's not depressing — that's empowering. Because it means you don't have to wait.

Second: brutal honesty. Don't lie to yourself about your effort. If you journal, don't write what sounds smart — write what's real. If you train, don't coast — push. If you screw up, admit it. Don't justify your failure. Extract the lesson and reload. This isn't about perfection. It's about honesty, alignment, and consistency.

Third: track everything. You don't rise to your goals — you fall to your systems. This Challenge isn't "try your best when you feel like it." It's binary. You either hit the task or you didn't. At the end of each day, you'll know if you won. And if you didn't — you'll know why. That kind of daily clarity is rare. Most men live in vagueness. This will snap you out of it.

This mindset is the foundation. Without it, you'll fall off by Day 4 and convince yourself the Challenge "just wasn't for me." That's soft talk. This is the real work. It's not about hype. It's about showing up when it's boring, hard, inconvenient, and messy — and doing it anyway. That's where the edge is built.

Weeks 1–2: The Core Pillars of Rebuilding

The first two weeks are about reclaiming what you've let slide — your mind, your body, your social presence, and your personal standard. These are the *Core 4* — the daily disciplines that every man needs sharp if he's going to lead his own life. Every day, you will hit all four. No skipping. No switching. This is about repetition with intention — what Navy SEALs call "deliberate discomfort." You're reprogramming your baseline.

1. MINDSET / MENTAL

You don't control your life until you control your mind. That starts with awareness. Most guys think they're logical — they're not. They're just running loops: negative self-talk, imagined failure, internal noise from a lifetime of criticism and distraction. You don't fix that with willpower. You fix it with *tools*.

Every morning, you'll journal. Not poetry. Not fluff. You'll sit down and ask yourself: What am I avoiding? What am I afraid of? Where am I lying to myself? This kind of writing isn't for content — it's for clarity. You bleed onto the page. That's how you start to surface what's actually running your behavior. A recent study from Harvard shows journaling boosts emotional regulation and executive function. That's science — but you'll feel it way before the data matters.

You'll also run self-talk drills. This means catching the inner critic in real time. When you hear the voice say "I'm tired," you don't fight it — you *reframe it*. You say, "Good. We train tired." You flip weakness into fuel. Over time, this becomes automatic. You stop negotiating with softness. You start leading your mind.

Finally: visualization. Every day, take 3–5 minutes to close your eyes and *see yourself* doing what needs to be done. This is not "manifestation." This is neurological rehearsal. Your brain builds familiarity through repetition — mental or physical. Athletes use this before games. Operators use it before missions. You'll use it every morning before the day hits you.

2. PHYSICAL

Your body is your base. Weak body, weak signal. You don't need to be a bodybuilder. But you *do* need to be strong, mobile, and disciplined. Every day of this Challenge includes physical training. You pick the modality — weights, calisthenics, combat sports, rucking, HIIT — but it must push you. No skipping. No minimal effort.

Why daily? Because momentum needs physical anchors. Your body is a thermostat. When it moves with intensity, your brain shifts out of passive mode. You build testosterone, dopamine, and internal fire. Studies show consistent training raises baseline energy and improves emotional regulation. Translation: when you train, you become harder to knock off balance.

You'll also build recovery discipline. Sleep window: 7+ hours. No devices 60 minutes before bed. Stretching or breathwork to downshift. Not because it's trendy — because your nervous system is wired for rhythm. You can't lead if you're drained.

And posture? You track it daily. No slouching. No weak eye contact. You carry yourself like you *know* who you are — not fake confidence, but trained presence. Most men's energy leaks through how they sit, stand, walk, or breathe. Fix this, and your confidence shifts without a word.

3. SOCIAL

This one gets ignored, but it's crucial. Social strength isn't about extroversion — it's about courage. Every day, you'll do one "courage challenge." That might mean making eye contact and holding it. Starting a conversation with a stranger. Giving a genuine compliment. Or calling someone you've been avoiding.

Why? Because most of your potential is being blocked by social fear. Fear of judgment. Fear of awkwardness. Fear of not being accepted. You kill that fear by *walking into it*. Repeated exposure rewires your social nervous system. You stop overthinking, and you start acting.

And beyond courage? Real connection. Every day, one *real* conversation. Not a meme DM. Not a two-second "yo." A moment where you check in with someone, ask something real, or say something that matters. We're not here to become fake socialites. We're here to become men who *lead* in relationships — with presence, not performance.

4. DISCIPLINE

This is the thread that ties it all together. Discipline isn't about restriction — it's about *direction*. You'll set three daily non-negotiables: wake time, phone use limit, and nutrition code.

Wake time is your anchor. Set it. Stick to it. No snoozing. No bargaining. Your morning sets your rhythm. Own it. Phone use must be intentional. Set limits on your apps. No scroll traps. No dopamine binges. Your mind is your tool — don't dull it first thing in the morning with randomness. Nutrition: pick a code and honor it. No fast food. No processed garbage. Hydrate. Eat like your performance depends on it — because it does.

Discipline isn't sexy. It's silent. And that's the point. When you get this dialed in, you stop feeling scattered. You stop playing catch-up. You start moving like a man who knows what time it is.

Tracking & Reflection — Logging Wins and Learning Fast

You'll log every single day of this Challenge. Not to feel good — to stay *honest*. Every night, answer these:

- Did I hit all four pillars?
- Where did I hesitate or compromise?
- What did I learn about myself today?

This isn't journaling for the sake of it. It's performance review. And you need it — because most guys never track anything. That's why they stay stuck. No feedback loop. No clarity. This challenge gives you a scoreboard. And over time, you'll start to notice patterns. When you slack. When you rise. What triggers you. What strengthens you.

You'll also learn how to *recover from setbacks*. Because they will happen. You'll oversleep. You'll miss a workout. You'll snap at someone, eat something trash, or go passive in conversation. Good. That's where the real training happens. The goal isn't to be perfect — the goal is to become *unbreakable*. That means learning how to take a hit, recalibrate, and get sharper the next day.

There's a reason the Navy SEALs use After Action Reviews. Because reflection is what makes failure useful. This Challenge trains that.

Weeks 3–4: Expansion, Mastery & Integration

The first two weeks of the Challenge are about resistance. Repetition. Getting back in the fight. But once you hit Day 15, something shifts. You stop forcing yourself to do the work — and you start becoming the man who does it. That's the power of rhythm.

Discipline is the tool you use when it's hard. Rhythm is what shows up when it becomes who you are. It's not habit for the sake of habit — it's identity. You wake up earlier without bargaining. You train without hype. You speak clearly without overthinking. You begin to move like a man who's not managing chaos — but *leading it*.

There's a line you'll cross somewhere between Day 15 and Day 21. At first, you won't notice it. One morning, the alarm goes off and you don't hesitate. A stranger starts small talk and you don't freeze. You look in the mirror and don't immediately criticize. That's not hype — that's evidence. You're rewiring who you are, not just what you do. But now the real game begins.

Advanced Drills — Week 3 and 4

Now that the foundation is set, we raise the stakes. No coasting. No "just enough." These final two weeks are about *expansion* — increasing pressure without losing precision. Here's how you go deeper in every domain:

MENTAL — Pressure Exposure & Stoic Fire

At this stage, journaling evolves. You're no longer just unpacking thoughts. You're sharpening your edge. You'll now write from a position of challenge. Use prompts that put you face-to-face with stress, ego, and discomfort:

- *Where am I still playing safe?*
- *What fears am I still hiding from?*
- *If someone followed me for 24 hours, would they respect my standard?*

This is Stoic journaling: stripping away illusion and preparing for impact. You write not to feel good, but to train clarity under fire. Like Marcus Aurelius writing in battle camps — not to impress, but to stay sharp. This mindset rewires your reactions. You stop needing control over the world and start developing control over yourself.

Next: *deliberate discomfort exposure.* Each day, you must *choose* something uncomfortable — not because you "have to," but because you *can.* Cold exposure. Hard conversations. Intense focus sessions with no music, no snacks, no dopamine. The point? Build your tolerance to psychological tension. You stop flinching. You stop needing stimulation. You build stillness in stress — and that's mental dominance.

114

PHYSICAL — Intensity + Precision

Your physical baseline is stronger now. That means it's time to push — but smarter, not louder. You don't just train harder — you train cleaner. This is where recovery becomes a weapon. You start treating your body like a system. Water intake. Sleep hygiene. Post-training downshift. You track what drains you and what fuels you. You build a *personal manual*.

Start practicing movement awareness — not just lifting heavy, but lifting *present*. Time your rest periods. Breathe between sets. Feel your posture under pressure. This isn't mindfulness for Instagram. This is how athletes recover faster, stay focused longer, and reduce injury risk. You're not here to just "work out" — you're here to train like your future depends on it.

You'll also implement "exit drills" — after your training session, you spend 5–10 minutes cooling down in silence. No phone. No talking. Just breath and presence. Why? Because transition discipline is the secret weapon most men ignore. If you can move from high-intensity to grounded calm without needing distraction, you're a dangerous man.

SOCIAL — Leadership Micro-Moments

By now, your social courage has risen. Time to evolve from confidence to *influence*. You start looking for what we call "leadership micro-moments" — tiny openings to lead without force. It's the way you give clear directions when others hesitate. The way you take responsibility in group settings without fanfare. The way you offer honest feedback when everyone else stays quiet.

These aren't about being alpha. They're about being *useful*. Powerful men don't seek control — they seek *service*. Your goal in every interaction is to bring clarity, calm, or forward momentum. You listen more than you speak, but when you speak — people move.

Practice *honest communication drills*. That means saying what you mean, clearly, with no filler. You don't hedge your tone. You don't soften your words out of fear. You speak with respect — but you don't apologize for being direct. Do this in text, in person, in email — everywhere. The world is starved for clean masculine communication. Be the man who brings it.

DISCIPLINE — Total Systemization

You've been keeping promises. Now we systemize them.

Morning and night are no longer random. You'll now lock in a *repeatable command structure*. Wake at the same time. Run the same first three actions. Create a non-negotiable evening protocol: screen cut-off, sleep downshift, and journaling. This becomes your daily operating system.

Next: kill *relapse habits* at the root. Look at your past 15 days. What still drags you back into softness? Is it phone scrolling? Late-night junk? Emotional reactions? Don't manage them — *eliminate* them. Set blockers, move apps, build friction. The more automatic your standards become, the more energy you free up to lead.

These two weeks are not about adding more. They're about *cutting the waste* and doubling down on what works. You're building a system that doesn't need hype to run — it just runs.

Common Crashes — And How to Respond Like a Pro

Here's where most men fall off.

Day 18 — you're tired.
Day 21 — you miss one task.
Day 24 — you want to quit and restart.

This is the point where amateurs tap out. They make one mistake and fall into a guilt spiral. "I ruined it." No. You didn't. You *tested the edge*. And now you respond like a professional.

A pro doesn't spiral. A pro *reviews*. What triggered the crash? What system failed? What adjustment is needed? Then he resets and returns with *more precision*. No drama. No self-pity. Just adaptation.

Your ego wants perfection. But growth comes from calibration.

This is why you track. This is why you reflect. So when the crash comes — and it *will* — you treat it like data, not identity. You don't lose momentum. You *redirect* it.

One hard truth: you will not "feel motivated" at this point. But that's good — because motivation is a distraction. This phase is where you harden your self-concept. You become

117

a man who acts, regardless of mood. That alone puts you in the top 5%.

Integration — Identity Is the Endgame

Here's the shift: you started this Challenge to *change your habits* — but by Week 4, it's your *self-image* that transforms.

This is the concept of **identity-based change**. In psychology, self-concept is the internal narrative of who you are. Most people try to change behavior first — but if the identity stays the same, old habits always return.

In this Challenge, you've stacked evidence every day: reps, wins, presence, consistency. You've created what James Clear calls *identity proof*. The more you act like the man you want to become, the more you start *being* him. This is where it gets quiet — but powerful. You stop needing external validation. You stop asking if you're "doing enough." You just *move*. Not because you're chasing something — but because this is your standard now. It's your *normal*.

You've built new neural pathways. You've hardened discipline into instinct. You've rewired your nervous system to seek challenge instead of avoid it. And most importantly — you've taught your mind to trust *you* again. That's what separates real transformation from another dopamine spike. You're not following a plan. You've become the plan.

After the 30 Days — Your Next Mission

This is not the end. It's the ignition point. You now have a system that works. You've stress-tested it. You've cut the noise. You've built rhythm. So, what do you do with it?

You *scale it.*

That could mean extending it into a 90-Day Mission. Same Core 4 — but with new intensity targets, new outcome goals, new discomfort zones. You're no longer just surviving the day — you're building something. Or you run a focused sprint: 14 days of total silence. A 21-day physical overload. A 30-day communication leadership challenge. You customize your evolution — but you *don't stop evolving.*

Keep the Core 4 as your baseline. Always. Track it. Refine it. Expand it. This becomes your *living code.*

The Challenge wasn't about 30 days. It was about *ownership.* Now you carry it forward. Quietly. Relentlessly. Cleanly.

The Oath

This isn't a program, a trend, or a 30-day dopamine hit. It's a code — and if you made it to the end, you've proven something rare: that when you stop negotiating with comfort, you become dangerous. You've stopped chasing motivation. You've started living with structure. You've built discipline through action, not theory. You've earned internal clarity without needing external applause.

You don't walk the same now. You don't speak the same. You carry a presence built from effort — not noise. And you don't have to explain it. People feel it. They adjust around it. Quietly. Instinctively.

If you didn't finish? You still know what the edge looks like now. You know where it breaks. That's your next starting point. Don't shrink from it. Step back in with more focus, less ego, and zero excuses.

The Chad Mindset isn't about hype or image. It's structure. Stillness. Strength. And service. It's the life of a man who knows who he is, acts with intention, and keeps his standards high whether anyone's watching or not.

You don't need to talk about it. You don't need to post about it. Just live it. Relentlessly. Quietly. Every day. You're either proving it — or you're not.

Now move.

The Chad Mindset Playbook (Part 1)

Core Principles & Mental Frameworks)

This isn't a summary. This isn't a motivational recap. This is the operating system — the mental software that turns every lesson in this book into real, daily behavior. If the rest of the book was the map, this is the compass. You don't refer to this once. You carry it. You run it. You live it.

The Chad Mindset isn't about becoming someone else. It's about stripping away everything that made you forget who you were — the excuses, the weak patterns, the distractions, the fear. And what's left? A man who moves with clarity. A man who doesn't need to dominate, but doesn't flinch. A man who isn't loud, but still leads the room. This chapter gives you the internal tools to become that man — not through hype, but through *mental structure.*

What the Playbook Is

You've gone through 16 chapters of fire. Discipline, physical training, mental reps, emotional control, clarity, social strength, stillness, leadership. All of it stacks. But unless it's wired into a simple mental code — you'll forget it. Or worse, you'll turn it into occasional hype with no integration.

That's what the Playbook is here to solve. This isn't about remembering ideas. It's about *installing frameworks.* So when life punches you in the face — you already know how to move.

We're building a mental operating system. One that doesn't depend on your mood. One that doesn't crash when life gets chaotic. One that turns pressure into precision.

Let's start at the foundation.

The Foundation Principles

1. Radical Ownership

You are not responsible for everything that happens to you. But you are responsible for how you meet it. Every time. No exceptions. Radical ownership is the act of eliminating blame — not out of guilt, but out of *power*.

You lost time? Own it.
You missed a workout? Own it.
You stayed in a job you hate for too long? Own that, too.

It doesn't mean you hate yourself. It means you're the kind of man who doesn't outsource responsibility to circumstance. That's freedom. That's where self-trust begins.

Ownership doesn't feel good in the moment. But it gives you back your spine. Victimhood is heavy. Ownership clears the weight. One clear decision at a time.

Mental Reframe: "This is mine. So is the solution."

2. The Hard Path Principle

Comfort is a liar. It tells you you're okay where you are. But you're not. You're just safe — and that's not the same as fulfilled.

The hard path is the true path. It's the one that calls you up, not down. It's uncomfortable, but it builds capacity. Want to get stronger mentally? Do things you don't want to do — on purpose. Want clarity? Sit with discomfort instead of escaping it.

Growth doesn't whisper. It punches.

The Hard Path Principle means choosing challenge daily. Not recklessly. But deliberately. It's why cold showers matter. Why hard conversations matter. Why putting your phone down and facing silence matters.

The pain of the hard path is real — but so is the pride.

Mental Reframe: "If it's hard, it's probably right."

3. Focus Is the New Strength

Modern men aren't weak. They're *scattered*. Their attention is bleeding out through every screen, app, tab, and notification. That's not a motivation problem. That's a bandwidth crisis.

Focus is the most valuable resource you have. Every decision, every habit, every result — it flows from your ability to stay locked in. Guard it like your life depends on it. Because it does.

You don't need to do more. You need to *do less better*. One task. One goal. One outcome. When you protect your focus, you become faster, sharper, calmer, and more dangerous. That's real power.

Mental Reframe: "Protect my focus. Starve everything else."

4. Identity Before Outcome

Most men chase goals thinking the result will change them. But transformation doesn't start with what you do — it starts with *who you believe you are*.

Want to build consistency? Become the kind of man who is consistent. Want discipline? Identify as someone who honors his word. That's how you act in alignment — because your behavior now matches your identity.

It's not wishful thinking. It's neural science. The more you behave like a man you respect, the more your brain rewires itself to believe that's who you are. This is where outcome-based motivation dies — and self-respect takes over.

Mental Reframe: "I don't chase results. I act in alignment."

Mindset Shifts That Rewire Behavior

Here's where the rubber meets the road. You don't need more "tools" — you need better *lenses*. These are the shifts that pull you out of passivity and into control. For each, you'll get a clear contrast, the logic behind it, and how to apply it daily.

Victim → Creator

The victim sees life as happening *to* him. The creator sees life as happening *through* him. The difference isn't just attitude — it's strategy. The victim waits for permission. The creator moves with initiative.

Drill: Catch every complaint in your head today and convert it into a choice. "This is unfair" becomes "What can I build from this?" You'll notice the mental energy shift almost instantly.

Real Example: You miss a promotion. Victim says, "They don't see my value." Creator says, "What can I build that forces them to?"

Distraction → Discipline

Distraction isn't just about phones. It's anything that disconnects you from presence. Most men use distraction to numb discomfort — but that discomfort is where the signal is.

Drill: Set a 60-minute block daily with zero stimulation: no phone, no music, no passive inputs. Force yourself to focus on one task, or to sit in silence and write. Watch what comes up.

Real Example: Instead of doomscrolling to avoid your anxiety, you face it, write about it, and then build a plan to move through it.

Approval → Self-Respect

Chasing validation is slavery in disguise. You post for likes. You speak to avoid conflict. You work to impress instead of express. It's exhausting. And it never ends.

Real power comes when your standard comes *from within*. Not from applause, not from praise. From the man in the mirror. If he's proud, you're good. If he's not — fix it.

Drill: Say no to something this week that you'd normally say yes to just to avoid conflict. Honor your standard. Let the discomfort build muscle.

Real Example: Turning down a social invite not because you're antisocial — but because your training, rest, or mission comes first.

Speed → Consistency

You've been lied to. Hustle isn't the key — consistency is. Most men start hard, flame out, and start again. Winners don't sprint — they *move daily*.

Consistency compounds. It's not loud. It's not sexy. But it builds identity, evidence, and momentum. That's what makes you unshakeable.

Drill: Choose one habit you've tried and dropped. Restart it today, but make it *smaller*. Stick to it for 30 days. No skips. Let the reps rebuild your self-trust.

Real Example: You used to meditate for 20 minutes, failed, and quit. Now you do 3 minutes every morning for 30 days straight — and now it sticks.

Mantras & Mental Scripts

The brain is a pattern-recognition machine. And patterns are built through repetition and *emotionally charged language*. That's where mantras come in — not as cheesy affirmations, but as *scripts* you program into your system.

Here are a few to install. Don't just repeat them. *Feel them.* Use them when you're tired, off-track, doubting yourself, or about to fold.

- **"No excuses. Only execution."** → Use when you're about to rationalize softness.
- **"Pain is proof I'm alive."** → Use when discomfort rises and you want to run.
- **"Decide. Move. Adjust later."** → Use when stuck in overthinking or hesitation.
- **"I don't rise to motivation. I fall to my standard."** → Use when discipline fades.

How to anchor them:

1. **Write them** every morning.
2. **Speak them** before a challenge or task.
3. **Reflect** on them each night — did you live them, or fold?

Over time, these mantras create neurological cues. When the moment hits, your default response becomes *power, not panic.*

Applied Psychology: Why This Works

Let's get clinical for a moment — because this isn't just mindset philosophy. This is cognitive science.

Your brain is plastic — not physically, but neurologically. It rewires itself based on repetition, emotional intensity, and reward. This process is called **neuroplasticity**, and it's what every part of this book has leveraged.

Every habit you've built over the last month — every rep, every journal, every time you faced resistance and didn't fold — all of it has created *new neural highways*. That's not theory. That's biology.

In neuroscience terms:

- **Dopamine** drives desire and momentum. When you stack small wins, dopamine reinforces those behaviors.
- **Myelin** is the insulation layer around neural pathways. Repetition strengthens it — which is why consistency makes action easier over time.
- **The Prefrontal Cortex** is your decision-making center. Mindfulness, focus drills, and daily routines reduce overload here, making you calmer under pressure.

You've not just been "changing habits." You've been rewiring your identity. The evidence is in how you move now — not perfectly, but purposefully. You're no longer reacting. You're *responding*. That's not positive thinking. That's *dominance by design*.

Transitioning Forward: From Mental Framework to Tactical Execution

Now you've got the internal OS. You've built the lens. You've coded the responses. But mindset alone isn't the game. It's the foundation.

The second half of this Playbook is where it gets applied — in *real-time decisions*. You'll learn how to walk into chaos and still move with clarity. How to handle rejection, failure, temptation, conflict, and pressure without dropping your standard. We'll cover social dynamics, daily decision rules, and what it means to lead yourself and others with silent authority. It's time to move from *internal wiring* to *external precision*. Let's turn the page.

The Chad Mindset Playbook (Part 2)

Tactical Application & Integration)

You've got the internal system now. Principles, mantras, mindset shifts — all wired. Now it's time to put it to work. Because mindset without execution is just another fantasy. You don't need more motivation. You need *rules that run under pressure* — when your brain goes foggy, your energy drops, or life punches you in the face. That's what this part of the Playbook is for: building *real-time systems* that make movement automatic. This is how you operate when thinking stops and action starts.

The "If-Then" Rules of Execution

Discipline dies in indecision. When you stop to question what to do — you've already lost time, momentum, and clarity. So instead, we pre-load behavior. We write the script in advance. If X happens, then I do Y. Simple. Clean. No drama.

These are your personal *decision codes* — rules that override emotion with movement.

- **If I feel fear → I move within 5 seconds.** Fear tolerated grows. Fear challenged shrinks. Your rule is to act *before* your brain can build excuses.
- **If I wake up tired → I start the day anyway.** Your feelings don't vote anymore. Your commitment does.

- **If I miss a day → I double the effort tomorrow with precision.** No guilt spirals. No "start over Monday." Just bounce back cleaner.

- **If I catch myself scrolling → I close it and return   to   the   mission.** Distraction loses its power the second you interrupt the loop.

- **If I feel resistance → I take it as a green light.** Resistance is your internal signal that the action matters. Move *toward* it.

Why does this work? Because the brain loves *certainty*. Pre-written rules remove negotiation. They eliminate the grey zone where discipline dies. And over time, these If-Then scripts become identity anchors. You don't even think about them anymore — they *are* you. Write your own. Tattoo them to your daily structure. And run them until they're automatic.

Domains of Mastery – Playbook in Action

You don't need ten systems. You need one mindset applied *everywhere*. Let's walk through the four real-world arenas where your Playbook becomes power — not theory.

1. Work & Business — Precision Over Noise

This isn't about becoming a hustle zombie. It's about strategic discipline. In your career, the Playbook means three things: ownership, consistency, and patience. You stop blaming your job, your boss, the market. You own your inputs. You show up even when no one claps. You think long, execute short — move daily, but with vision.

Example: You're behind on a deadline. The weak move is panic or hiding. The Playbook move is to breathe, clarify your top three priorities, and communicate clearly. Ownership + calm execution = respect.

Drill: End each workday with a "Shutdown Sequence": Log the three wins, three lessons, and your next three tasks. This builds closure and reduces mental clutter.

You're not chasing hustle highs anymore. You're building leverage — one focused block at a time.

2. Body — Discipline Beyond the Gym

Training is no longer optional. It's not a hobby. It's your daily anchor.

The Playbook doesn't care if it's a rest day, travel day, or bad mood day — your standard is movement. Even 20 minutes. Even bodyweight. You don't ask *if* you'll train. You ask *how* you'll train today. But it goes further. You don't just train hard. You recover hard. You hydrate. You sleep like it's sacred. You stretch without skipping. You eat like your testosterone depends on it — because it does.

Drill: Add a "Posture Audit" every hour during the day. Back straight. Chin neutral. Shoulders back. It rewires not just confidence, but how your nervous system fires.

Example: You're exhausted at 9 p.m. Stillness wants junk food and Instagram. The Playbook move? Brush your teeth early. Chug a glass of water. 10 deep nasal breaths. Bed. Not sexy — but lethal.

You don't need to look like a model. You need to look in the mirror and respect the machine.

3. Social — Lead Without Performing

Confidence isn't noise. It's *clarity under pressure.*

In social situations, the Playbook removes performance. You're not there to impress. You're there to *connect honestly or lead directly.* You don't pretend to be alpha. You stay grounded. You speak clearly. You listen with presence. And when tension hits — you don't fumble. You hold your frame.

If-Then Rule: If the room gets tense → slow your breath and hold eye contact. You don't flinch. You let the room calibrate to *you.*

Drill: Daily "Social Rep": Start one real conversation per day — no scripts, no agenda. Just direct presence.

Example: Someone challenges your opinion in public. The weak move is overexplaining. The Playbook move? Hear it. Pause. Say what you mean without defending. Let silence do the work. In a world full of overreactors, your calm is leadership.

4. Purpose — From Random Hustle to Aligned Action

You're not here to grind forever. You're here to *build something aligned.* That requires two things: a mission you believe in, and daily actions that serve it. The Playbook teaches that *clarity beats passion*. You don't wait for purpose to strike you like lightning. You define what matters — then you act like it's sacred.

Drill: Weekly "Mission Audit." Ask:

- What am I building?
- What actions this week directly moved that mission forward?
- What distractions cost me energy with no return?

You're no longer doing "productive things" to feel busy. You're moving with design. You're building a legacy, not just checking boxes.

If-Then Rule: If a task doesn't serve your top 3 priorities → delegate it, delay it, or delete it.

Your purpose isn't a quote on your wall. It's the filter for how you use your time, focus, and energy.

Staying in Command Under Pressure

You've built structure. But pressure will still hit — stress, emotion, setback, chaos. The difference now is you don't collapse. You regulate. You return to *command mode* fast. Here's how:

1. Crisis Breathing

When your nervous system floods, the mind spins. Reset through your body.

Try this: *4-2-6 protocol*

- Inhale through the nose for 4 seconds

- Hold for 2
- Exhale slowly through the nose for 6

Do this for 2 minutes when overwhelmed. It flips your body from sympathetic (fight-flight) to parasympathetic (calm-focus).

2. Reframing Adversity

Pressure is neutral. It's your story about it that breaks you.

The Playbook reframe:

- "This is happening *for* me."
- "This is a test of who I said I want to become."
- "This isn't chaos — it's training."

You shift from victim to operator. Pressure becomes data. You adapt, not react.

3. Command Mode Reset

Create a physical ritual to reset your state fast. Could be:

- Splashing cold water on your face.
- Standing tall and adjusting posture.
- Saying a single mantra aloud: *"Reset. Lead."*

This creates an anchor. Your body gets the signal: "We're back in control."

The Integration Loop

You don't just set rules and forget them. You refine them. Weekly. That's how professionals operate.

Here's your loop:

- **Sunday Review:** What rules worked? What broke? What got missed?
- **Refine:** Do your If-Then rules need adjusting? Any friction to remove?
- **Recommit:** Re-read your personal Playbook. Out loud. With presence.
- **Identity Stack:** End by journaling this: *"Who am I becoming? What proof did I build this week?"*

You're not chasing streaks. You're reinforcing *identity*. That's what makes the Playbook stick. That's what makes it real when life gets loud. This isn't about discipline for 30 days. It's about building a *mental code* that carries for life.

Living the Playbook

You won't always feel on. You won't always win the day. That's not the point. The point is that you now have *a standard*. One that doesn't move when emotions do. One that protects your focus, your time, your energy. One that makes you move cleaner, speak clearer, and live sharper.

You've built a mindset that can lead under pressure. A nervous system that doesn't flinch. A physical body that earns self-respect. And a mental code that silences excuses before they even form. There's no final test. No trophy. Just *you* — every morning — choosing to either live the Playbook or fold into noise. And that's where the quiet confidence comes from.

Recommended Tools & Resources

Most guys fall into one of two traps: either they chase tools hoping they'll *fix* them, or they ignore them completely and try to white-knuckle everything alone. Both are wrong.

The right tools don't replace the work. They sharpen it. They cut friction. They reinforce the mindset and structure you've built through this book. That's what this list is — a filtered set of resources that serve the mission. Nothing extra. Nothing that adds noise.

You don't need to download everything here. You don't need to read them all at once. This isn't homework — it's a toolbox. Come back to it when something breaks, slows down, or needs upgrading.

These aren't chosen because they're popular. They're chosen because they work for men committed to self-respect, mental clarity, physical strength, and disciplined living.

Books — For Your Mindset and Mission

These aren't motivational fluff. These are mindset recalibrators. Read them with a highlighter. Revisit them when you drift. Each one teaches a mental law you'll live by.

- **Meditations – Marcus Aurelius -** Timeless, tested, and raw. A Roman emperor journaling through war, loss, and duty — while staying grounded. This is stoic self-leadership at its core. Read slowly. Read often.

- **Can't Hurt Me – David Goggins** - A modern blueprint for mental toughness. No excuses, no filters — just what happens when you stop being soft and start taking full ownership of your pain.

- **The War of Art – Steven Pressfiel -** You don't need more goals — you need to kill resistance. This short, punchy book is a daily slap in the face for anyone avoiding their real work.

- **Deep Work – Cal Newport -** Focus is a weapon. This shows how to protect and direct it in a world designed to distract you into mediocrity.

- **Atomic Habits – James Clear** - Not about motivation. About building systems. Identity-first thinking, habit stacking, and small wins that compound.

- **The Way of Men – Jack Donovan** - A controversial but important breakdown of primal masculinity, tribe, strength, and male initiation. Take the value, skip the ego.

- **Military Workout – ZEP –** Military workouts are great exercises to shape both the body and the mind.

🎙 Podcasts — Sharpen While You Move

These voices are sharp, grounded, and consistent. No fake guru energy. Just men thinking, leading, and delivering lessons that stick.

- **Jocko Podcast – Jocko Willink** - War stories, extreme ownership, and how to lead under pressure. You'll walk away ready to handle anything.

- **The Tim Ferriss Show** - Tactical breakdowns from world-class performers. Skip the small talk — pull out the frameworks that apply to your mission.

- **Modern Wisdom – Chris Williamson** - Smart conversations on masculinity, mental clarity, relationships, and living well in a distracted world.

- **Andrew Huberman Podcast** - Neuroscience meets discipline. Sleep, focus, cold exposure, dopamine — this is your brain, upgraded.

📺 YouTube — Learn in Action

When you need visual reinforcement — form, philosophy, or fire — these channels deliver. No fluff. No endless ads. Just impact.

- **Mark Bell / Mind Bullet / Power Project** - Masculine strength, no BS. Learn from pros about lifting, recovery, hormone health, and self-respect.

- **Hamza** - For younger men escaping porn, video games, and social media addiction. Raw and imperfect, but a solid push out of modern weakness.

- **Jeff Nippard** - Science-based training done right. No ego, no shortcuts. Just clean instruction that works long-term.

- **Chris Williamson Clips** - Short, sharp segments on mindset, relationships, status, and performance. Easy to digest, hard to forget.

📱 Apps — Automate Discipline & Kill Noise

If your phone's a problem, use it as a weapon. These apps remove temptation, boost focus, and help you track what actually matters.

- **Streaks (iOS)** - Habit building made visual. Pick 4–6 non-negotiables and reinforce them with momentum.

- **Freedom / OneSec** - Hard block or soft interrupt. Both reduce mindless scrolling and train awareness.

- **Cold Turkey (Desktop)** -Blocks anything that kills focus. Great for deep work or writing sessions.

- **Rise** - Understand your sleep debt, energy cycles, and when your brain's most locked in.

- **Notes (iOS/Mac default)** - Still the best tool for quick thoughts, reflection, and journaling. Simplicity wins.

🔧 Gear — Low-Tech Tools for High-Discipline Living

Minimalism isn't about owning nothing. It's about owning *only what strengthens you*. These are simple tools that reinforce posture, presence, and physical edge.

- **Weighted Vest (20–40 lbs)** - No time? Walk with weight. Push-ups, squats, stairs — all instantly harder. Builds physical and mental grit.

- **Foam Roller / Lacrosse Ball** - Mobility and recovery tools that cost nothing but save you years of pain and tightness.

- **Red Light / Blue Light Glasses** - Optional — but if you're staring at screens late, protect your circadian rhythm and testosterone.

- **Noise-Canceling Headphones** - Silence isn't a luxury. It's a focus multiplier. Cut the chatter — stay on task.

- **Analog Watch** - Stop pulling your phone out 100x a day. You only need to know the time. Reclaim your focus.

Final Note: Don't Collect: USE

Most men get stuck in the trap of *resource hoarding*. They think reading five more books will fix them. Or that downloading every productivity app will magically make them focused. Or that following the right influencers will somehow transfer discipline through osmosis. That's not how any of this works. The Chad Mindset isn't built through collection — it's built through execution. And execution only happens when your mindset is right going in.

So here's the mindset you carry with these tools: **you are not here to be entertained. You're here to be sharpened.** Whether it's a book, a podcast, a video, or an app — you are not the consumer. You are the commander. The moment you hit play or turn the first page, your mission is to extract, apply, and reinforce. Not passively soak it in and feel smarter. That's empty fuel. You want *real-world carryover*. You want knowledge that leaves the screen and shows up in your habits.

When you read a book — you don't highlight for the dopamine of "doing something." You highlight to install. That means stopping after a key insight, sitting with it, maybe even journaling it in your own words. You don't skim a page just to say you "read today." You chew on sentences like they're protein. One-page applied in our everyday life beats 50 pages forgotten.

Same with podcasts. Don't binge them back-to-back while multitasking and forget everything an hour later. Choose one, listen fully, and walk away with a single concept to apply that day. If it's a mental framework, run it. If it's a question, journal on it. If it's a quote, repeat it. Lock it in. When you treat input like training, you stop wasting time pretending to improve.

Apps and gear are the same. A cold exposure tracker means nothing if you ignore it. A habit app doesn't build discipline unless you tie it to actual behavior. This chapter gave you clean, focused recommendations. But even the best tool becomes noise if you don't build rules around how and when you'll use it. So, build those rules. Define why you're using something. Set a time. Set a purpose. Run it like a drill — then move on.

And if a tool starts to create more distraction than discipline? Cut it. No drama. No guilt. Just a clean decision. You don't owe loyalty to anything that doesn't serve your mission. That includes books everyone praises but do nothing for you. That includes "influencers" who used to light a fire in you but now just waste your time with reels. That includes every shiny productivity tool that makes you feel busy while you avoid your actual work.

The point is not to be a minimalist for the sake of it. The point is to be *precise*. That's the mindset. Precision. You're not out here throwing random ideas against the wall hoping something sticks. You're building a machine. Every input has a purpose. Every resource has to earn its place in your system. And that system? That's what keeps you sharp when motivation fades and chaos hits.

So don't scroll through this chapter looking for a hack. Don't chase more tools hoping they'll do the work for you. Pick one thing that aligns with your current mission. Use it with intention. Apply it like a weapon. See if it earns its place. If it doesn't, discard it.

Conclusion

There's no finish line here. No credits rolling. No final boss to defeat. Just you — standing a little taller, moving a little cleaner, and carrying a different kind of silence inside.

What you've built isn't a persona. It's a foundation. It's the ability to meet life without flinching. The strength to do what needs to be done without broadcasting it. The clarity to act without asking for permission. Somewhere along the way, you stopped chasing transformation and started living it — not by changing who you are, but by remembering who you were supposed to be.

The world outside hasn't changed. It's still loud, soft, overstimulated, and confused. But now you see it differently. You don't take it personally anymore. You don't rush to react. You move from center. You decide where your attention goes, and you protect it like oxygen. That's what makes you rare. Not perfection — composure. Not noise — presence.

You know now that being a man isn't about domination or image. It's about *direction*. It's about waking up with purpose and going to bed with peace, knowing your actions match your words. It's about control — not of others, but of yourself. You've learned to own your thoughts, command your emotions, and steer your energy with intent. And that makes you dangerous in the best possible way.

This isn't about staying motivated. It's about staying *centered*. The fire will fade sometimes. The drive will stall. But the code remains. The Chad Mindset was never meant to hype you up — it was meant to anchor you down. To give you structure in chaos, stillness in pressure, and strength in simplicity.

So where do you go from here? Forward — quietly. You don't announce your evolution. You live it. You build, protect, and lead with calm aggression. You don't need to post about discipline or talk about purpose. You embody it. The world doesn't need another loud man trying to prove something. It needs grounded men building something that lasts.

There's a difference between being seen and being felt. You've spent enough time trying to be seen. Now it's time to be *felt*. No applause. No validation. No finish line. Just a quiet shift — permanent, disciplined, unstoppable. The Chad Mindset isn't a phase. It's not a program. It's a way of operating. Carry it forward. Refine it. Pass it on. Live like a man who no longer needs to say he's one.